ONLY DEAD FISH SWIM WITH THE CURRENT

Come Swim with me

Bill

Come Surfin with me

Bill

ONLY DEAD FISH SWIM WITH THE CURRENT

A memoir filled with wit and candour, exploring everything from a boyhood in Ireland to an adulthood overseas

BILL JERMYN

This book is memoir. It reflects the author's present recollections of experiences over time. Some names and characteristics have been changed, some events have been compressed, and some dialogue has been recreated.

Print ISBN: 978-1-7389619-0-0
eBook ISBN: 978-1-7389619-1-7

Front Cover photo: Author at Crookhaven, 1975
Back Cover photo: Altar Church, Toormore

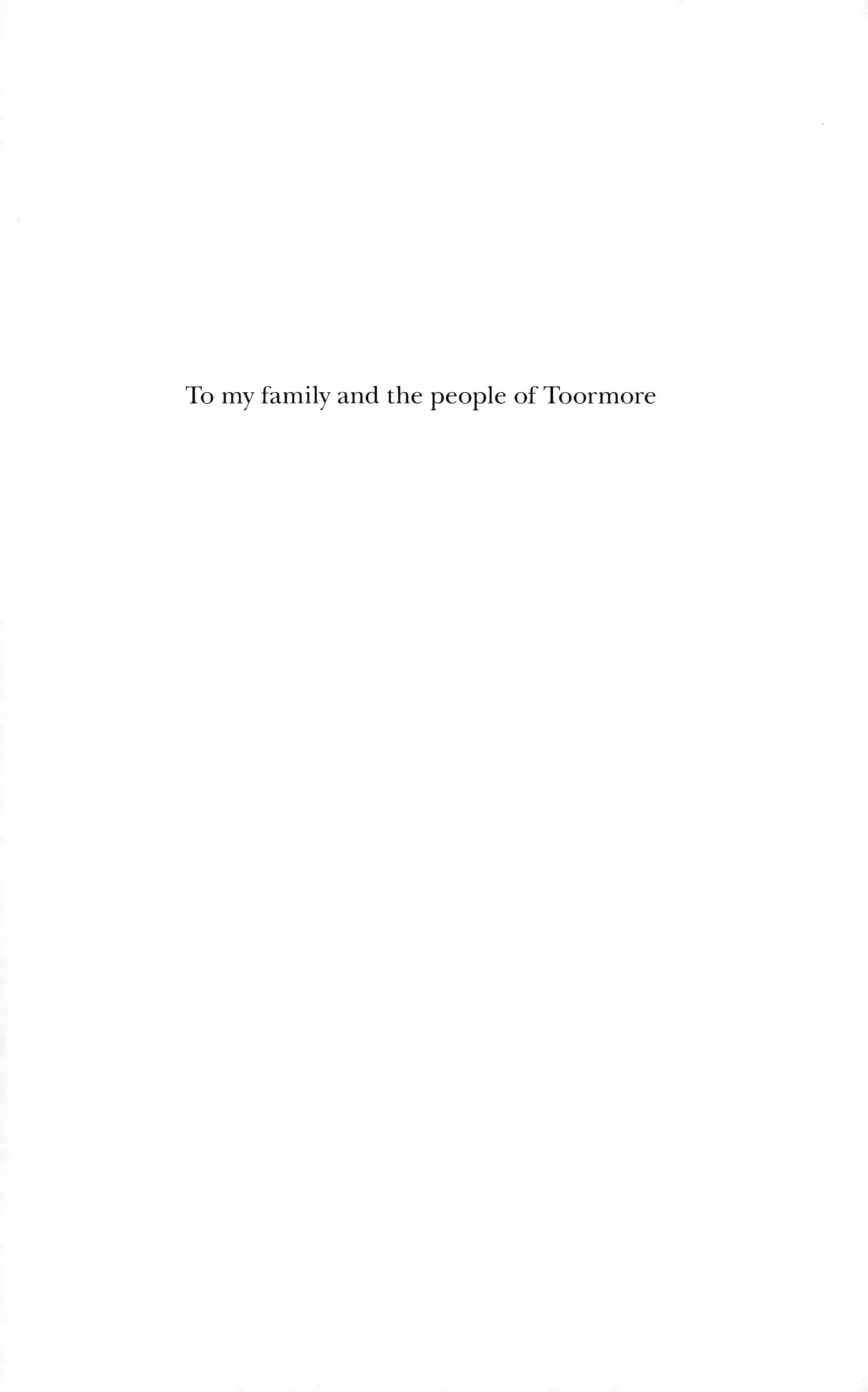

To my family and the people of Toormore

TABLE OF CONTENTS

INTRODUCTION

For years, I have related to the image of "Only dead fish swim with the current." While, like most, I have spent much time swimming with the current, I have often striven to turn against the flow, if not fully, at least ninety degrees. This memoir accounts for some of these efforts.

The book consists of tales of my childhood in Ireland and short visits to the Middle East and Africa as a young adult, as well as two years living in New York, from the nineteen-fifties through to the eighties.

I have made the manuscript North American-friendly in terms of common words and turns-of-phrase, but I have retained English spelling. I don't expect North Americans to be familiar with the details of the politics I mention from time to time, and so I will give a very brief outline here.

The island of Ireland has been populated for thousands of years by a variety of races, the most recent being the Celts, since about 600 BC. It was colonized by the English in the late eleven-hundreds.

The Unionists of Northern Ireland today are descended from a Protestant plantation from Scotland, in the late sixteen-hundreds.

After much violence, the Republic of Ireland in the south was formed in 1922, giving independence from the UK. However, the Unionists would not leave the union with the UK, and Northern Ireland was set up as an independent country within the UK. One of the unreconciled problems was a significant percentage of the population of Northern Ireland was of Catholic and Nationalist allegiance.

In the late sixties, violence broke out again, led by the IRA (nationalists, fighting the British) and responded to with violence by the British Army and Unionist (pro-British) terrorist groups. This period was euphemistically called "The Troubles." Finally, in 1998, the key leaders agreed to a ceasefire and signed the Good Friday Agreement.

Ever since, there has been an uneasy peace. The nationalists are now calling for a referendum on a united Ireland, while the Unionists (UK nationalists) are adamant they do not want to break their 400-year link to the UK. The UK government has promised it will offer a referendum on the issue (with a parallel referendum in the Republic) if it believes there is a reasonable chance of the result favouring a united Ireland. The latest census indicates that there are now more Catholics than Protestants in Northern Ireland, but allegiances don't go strictly by religion anymore. The problem remains: two sets of nationalists but with different loyalties, while there is an increasing number declaring as neither nationalist nor unionist, and these may be the hope for the future.

TOORMORE

1

HOME

If asked where precisely I come from, I answer by recounting the following story: during the Great Famine in Ireland in the 1840s, the potato crops failed, and with no other means of sustenance, the population starved and many were evicted.

A million died and another million emigrated to North America, some dying on the way. In the middle of this horror, the Catholic bishop of Cork in the south toured West Cork, one of the worst famine-stricken areas, to see the destitution for himself. On reaching the town of Schull, he was so horrified by the human misery he had encountered, he couldn't take any more. Instead of continuing his planned journey another fifteen miles to the end of the peninsula, he rode his horse to the top of the steep hill on the west side of the town, raised his hand, and said, "Bless all who live west of here."

That is where I come from— "west of here"— and I have always felt blessed.

I grew up just over a hundred years later, in the nineteen-fifties, in a small townland called Toormore. Located five miles west of Schull, ten miles short of the most south-westerly point in Ireland, it was my father's and paternal grandparents' home place. As you travel west from Schull, the road emerges from a rocky and boggy environment and opens up to Toormore Bay on the left and the Altar Stone, a pre-historic structure that has withstood the storms of time. The road goes down a small hill and passes the Altar Church on the right with the sea on the left. Then, the community water pump, followed by a long hill at the top of which the Jermyn home is on the left. The house is long and low, two-stories at right angles to the road, with an extension from the back facing the road. My parents ran a general grocery shop from there.

Toormore consisted of a drawn-out cluster of houses, a shop, and a church; the soothing noise of the sea was a constant. The population, diminished since the Famine, was less than fifty. We had no running water, no sewerage, no electricity, no telephone, and no paved roads. These amenities had arrived in Schull, but all those who were blessed to live "west of here" had to wait. However, as a child, I didn't feel I wanted for any of this; I had the freedom to wander wherever I wished with the other kids and we invented our own games.

My father built a new outhouse when I was a child in the early fifties that stood proudly on a hillock behind our home. I went there every morning before school. The smell was consistent and comforting with familiarity. As I got older, I enjoyed looking at some of the random news items from the neatly cut squares of newspaper curated by my father. I would read something about the war in Korea followed by news about a local man imprisoned for stealing a bicycle, and then a square with a food recipe, or the Suez Crisis. This method of absorbing an eclectic range of information fueled my thirst for knowledge. The morning ritual was a good way to get my head in gear for the day ahead.

My brother Richard (Rich) was over a year older than me. We did everything together, clad in identical corduroy pants down to the knees, and often in light-brown polo-neck sweaters. He never pulled rank, and there was never a fight of significance between us. We played endless cars and trucks on the pathways that traversed the rocky hillocks surrounding our and the neighbours' houses. We would chug along the pathways using the covers from floor polish tins for driving wheels, all the while issuing the sound of engines punctuated by honking horns and screeching brakes. We dug up corners and some straightaways to make them more passable, and sometimes we hacked open new roadways across the rocks, spending many happy hours at this pursuit.

Rich and I shared two outdoor chores from when we were five or six years old. We had three cows that needed to be taken to, and collected from, their grazing grounds daily. We owned a field way up through the rocks on the hill. The pathway went along by near-vertical rock where there was room for only single file. The final rock hurdle led to our field on the right. While the cows knew the route and there was little opportunity to go off course, our presence was important to ensure they got in to and out of the field.

Collecting drinking water from the pump at the bottom of the hill was the other chore. Bringing a bucket of water uphill was a challenge for small children. If I filled the bucket too full it would splash into my shoes. It became easier when we graduated to bicycles as we could walk the bicycles up the hill with the bucket of water hanging on the handlebars. However, if we were not careful, the bucket would bang against the bicycle frame and risk a major spill.

Our family regularly went for a Sunday cycle. Rich had a beautiful red bike, my mother rode in a sedate u-shaped High-Nelly, and my father had what was an unheard-of luxury at that time, a drop-handled sports bike. At first, I used to ride on his crossbar with my feet on the lamp bracket, which I loved. When I grew old enough to ride a bike and too big to fit comfortably on my father's, my parents could not afford another one for me, so we used to borrow a small bike from a neighbour's child. The trouble was that he was an only child who had every toy in the world, yet sometimes, at the last minute, he would refuse to allow me to take it. This caused me unspeakable grief since I then had to ride on the carrier behind my mother, which was embarrassing for someone my age.

The roadsides were covered in a profusion of wildflowers; purple heather and yellow gorse made a colourful blanket on the hills and rocks in spring. In the summer, the purple and scarlet fuchsia added to the palette, and in August the vibrant orange of montbretia dazzled my senses. The roadside and hills were on fire with the spectacle. The fuchsia had a lovely perfumed scent, and I regularly picked a flower and broke off the base to suck its sweet liquid. Few, other than the bees, knew this secret.

The cuckoo arrived in May. Its song was invigorating and unique—unique because it sounded like the word 'cuckoo,' the first syllable high and the second low—cuck-oo, cuck-oo. She repeated the call several times before going silent for a period and then commenced again.

Through all of this, I rarely saw the cuckoo. I would look all around when I heard her but could not be sure if I saw her. In May, her voice was throaty as if she was fighting a cold, and then it became clear as a flute in June before she disappeared for another year. Her song was the sweetest and purest in our bird kingdom and I stood transfixed whenever she started to sing. The mystique, of course, was increased by the story that she doesn't make her own nest, but rather pushes the eggs out from another bird's nest and claims it for herself.

The corncrake was another unusual bird, and it too was named after its strange voice; she called out, "crake, crake" from the cornfield in which she nested and lived. Her voice was not melodic like the cuckoo. Again, I never saw the bird but during the summer she thrilled me with her distinctive, scraping, deep call. She made her nest on the ground in the corn or hay fields and was concealed as the crops grew.

We had two beaches within walking distance from the house. My father taught me to swim in the larger one that was long and shallow with no waves.

"We'll start with the doggy paddle," he said.

Spluttering, I mastered that fairly quickly.

"Now for the breaststroke," he said.

"I keep sinking," I moaned.

"Keep at it and you will succeed," he said, as he demonstrated again.

He was a good swimmer, unusual for his generation who tended to view these water escapades as high risk/low return and for tourists only. Later, when I had mastered a few basic strokes, I often went to the other beach that was on a narrow and deep inlet and was ideal for swimming, either from the rocks or from the short, steep beach.

The constant movement and sound of the sea were always in the background if you listened. I spent many hours on the rocks in Toormore Bay watching the crash of the waves. I had a special rock I went to regularly in summer and winter. The small island in front of me, Carraig Mor—Big Rock—hosted flocks of cormorants which stood up straight with their long black necks, like sentries guarding their home. The repetitive pounding of the waves was a balm for my soul and gave me a sense of the continuity of the wider universe and our small part in it.

2

CARRIGMANUS

There was one other place that played a big part in my youth. It was Carrigmanus, where my maternal grandmother and my uncle Dick lived.

The flowery china washbowl, water jug, and chamber pot that sit on my bedroom dresser are a portal to the past. They come from my grandmother's farmhouse at Carrigmanus and are from the room where my mother slept as a girl. It is also where I was born.

When my mother was pregnant with me, she went to Carrigmanus and stayed there until after my birth. Her oldest sister, my aunt May, a midwife, presided over the occasion, and in the absence of baby-friendly paraphernalia, she placed me in a drawer from the large chest in the room. This had been the girls' bedroom, which my aunt Sadie and my mother shared for many years. Sadie was the youngest of my mother's siblings and was the last to be born here before me.

My first memory of Carrigmanus was a visit to my grandfather. He was sitting by the stove in the large kitchen with the stump of one leg stretched out on a stool like a felled tree. He'd had gangrene after some untreated infection, and amputation below the knee had been the recommended solution. That is the only memory I have of him. He died of a heart attack soon afterwards on Christmas Day, 1953.

Carrigmanus, the home of my mother's family, the Roycrofts, was a large farmhouse nestled in the side of a hill that sloped slowly down to Barley Cove, a golden-sanded beach that was popular for swimming. At the back of the house was a series of out-houses for cows, calves, and other animals, and a car garage with a work-pit in the middle that my uncle Dick used for repairs. He had an Alf Alfa sign from a Swedish milking machine fixed like a prized trophy to the front of the garage, as he was the first in the region to install a milking machine.

The main room in the house was the large kitchen. The window looked out over the front lawn, and onwards to Barley Cove in the distance. Opposite the window was the rack—a long wooden seat with a top that opened and gave access to storage space underneath. At one end, the old stove radiated constant heat from burning wood and coal. The undeniable focus of the room, however, was the narrow table under the window. It was the longest table I had ever seen, with stools for sitting stretching the length of each side.

After my grandfather died, my mother felt that my grandmother could do with some company to keep her spirits up. Rich wasn't keen to go but at that time, although no more than four years old, I volunteered. My grandmother, Granny Manus, was a small, rotund woman, but to me, she was a large and imposing figure. She went for a nap every afternoon and forced me to do the same. "Are you asleep yet?" she would call out as I lay in a cot beside her bed. I resisted the temptation to answer.

"Did you sleep?" she'd ask, as we were getting up again. Sometimes I did, sometimes I didn't, but I learned to pretend I did to avoid further interrogation and possible punishment.

In general, my memories of that stay with Granny Manus were good. I helped cut seed potatoes in a musty and undecorated upstairs room at the back of the house. Granny and several local women squatted on their haunches and cut the potatoes at a speed I could not equal. The sprouting potatoes would have two to four long sprouts, which we separated for planting. They exchanged gossip, or as much as would be said with a child present. Cutting seed was an annual social ritual for these women.

At a later time in spring, I helped with the planting. Uncle Dick, who had become my hero, used the tractor and plough to build up rows of parallel ridges, and all the rest of us planted the cut potatoes, row after row. Uncle Dick had the family good looks with the foreign influence of sallow skin and jet-black hair. The family was Protestant (Anglican), descended from Huguenots who were persecuted in France, some of whom took refuge in Ireland in the late 1600s. The whole family, including my mother, was dark-skinned with black hair. Some said there could be Spanish blood mixed in there also, due to the fact that there were survivors of Spanish Armada shipwrecks off the coast who landed and remained in West Cork. Whatever his origin, Dick was a wizard with machinery and one of the few who owned a car at the time.

Granny Manus had one ritual that was essential—listening at 6:00 p.m. every evening to the "Archers," a soap opera on BBC radio and unique in that it was based on farming characters. The large wireless was on a high shelf to the right of the stove and above the rack. We had to be there at about 5:45 p.m. to be sure to be ready; it took a while for the valves to heat up. When the well-loved actor Walter Gabriel's gravelly Midlands-accented voice filled the airwaves, Granny Manus was transported.

Like Toormore, indoor plumbing had not yet reached this area. In the typical outhouse, there was a large bucket inserted under a wooden seat, and cut newspaper squares served for toilet paper. On account of Granny having had a large family—four boys and four girls—when they were children, they were awarded the status of a large three-hole communal toilet, to ease the rush in the morning before school. Furthermore, it was cleverly built over a stream, so in a sense, this was one of the first flushing toilets in the area.

Eventually, I got sick with the mumps and my mother came to see me in Granny's darkened bedroom. I hadn't been thinking about or missing home, as I had been enjoying the adventure of living on a farm. However, all the news from Toormore made me think I was missing out, and so I asked to go home again.

I stayed two months and don't know whether I was any use to Granny Manus, because at that age I had no concept of her grief for my dead grandfather. During my stay with her and Uncle Dick, I developed a special bond with them and with the house itself.

3

JERMYN FAMILY

I spent a lot of my youth defending the allegation, "Jermyn, that's not a very Irish name." This was a subtle way of asserting, "You are a Protestant," or "nasty Protestant," depending on whether the interlocutor was merely clarifying information or implying a lesser being. I resented this stigmatization at the time but later in life came to recognize it as one of the factors that contributed to my "outsider" personality. I have never traced the family origin beyond knowing that my great-grandfather settled as a farmer in the next townland to the north of Toormore. He came from Ballydehob area, a small town about ten miles east of Toormore and the hub of the Jermyn settlement in West Cork.

My grandfather, Richard, also known as Dick, was a stonemason who came to Toormore around the turn of the twentieth century to start his married life. He married Bess Williamson from the townland and settled in a house in a beautiful little valley off the main road near the Altar church. In this idyllic setting, my father Tom, and Aunt Mary, also known as May, were born.

Soon afterwards the family moved 'uptown,' where Dick built a new home with a shop at one side. Some said he included the shop to give Bess something to do while he was away building. By all accounts, Dick was a gentleman and a joker with a great sense of humour, while Bess had delusions of grandeur; and never stopped complaining to Dick about everything, including her aches and pains. She would take her favoured customers into the kitchen for tea, but when the Musgraves, her main Cork suppliers, visited, they would be treated to the drawing room with Bess in all her finery. She had a strong sense of class and where she stood in the pecking order.

My aunt May died in her mid-twenties. My father never spoke about it. From a neighbour, I found out that she had hormonal development problems and Bess took her to the hospital in Cork, where she had an operation and died. Dick was consumed with grief when he got the news, claiming he was never told nor had given permission for her to have an operation. He went to Cork and brought her coffin home and opened it himself in the drawing room for his private farewell. He was incensed by what had happened and the neighbour told me that he never got over the loss.

Despite this tragedy, the family was prosperous early on. Apart from the building work and the shop, at various times Dick ran a grain mill, a produce collection service, and a hearse.

Slowly, during the forties, the family's wealth slipped away. With the advent of cooperative creameries, independent wholesalers could no longer compete. Also, the second World War put a damper on commercial activity. Bess continued her high-living ways even as Dick grew too old to work. While my father had many strengths, commercial acumen was not one of them, and by the time I arrived, there was little money to spare.

4

MY FATHER

My father, Tom, was born in 1902. He was as quiet as my mother was talkative, so I mostly remember things he did rather than what he said. Then again, because he spoke so little, I tend to remember much of what he said too.

"What are you asking?" the cattle buyer asked Dad.

"Thirty pounds," said Dad.

"Twenty pounds," the buyer retorted, "not a penny more," at which point Dad shook his head and the buyer walked on to inspect the next cows on the street nearby.

We were at the monthly Fair Day in Goleen. We had walked in the early morning from our home four miles away, he in front with the rope, and me with a stick behind our cow. Farmers were lining their cattle at each side of the short one-street village. The cattle buyers from far distant places strutted up and down, hectoring and bargaining until deals were done. The same buyer came and went to and from Dad a few more times, with neither budging from their positions. Each pretended to be less interested than the other. "Split the difference," the buyer said, "I'll settle for twenty-five pounds."

"Twenty-seven pounds, ten shillings," Dad responded.

It was evident by now that he had chosen a good starting price, and the buyer was interested. After much mutterings about breaking each other out of house and home, and Dad threatening to take the cow home again, the buyer capitulated. The deal was sealed with the buyer spitting on his hand and engaging in an exaggerated handshake. As we made the long walk home, I could see from the smile on his face that he was well pleased with his day's work.

Dad was a striking figure, six-feet-tall, already bald, with a long thin nose and classical good features. In his early twenties, he bought the first Model T Ford truck in the region. To be successful with this, not only did he need to be able to drive, but also to take it apart, fix it, and put it together again. Once he'd driven out of the dealership in Skibbereen—a large town twenty miles away—there was nowhere, or no one, who could help if something went wrong. He stayed a few days in the Eldon Hotel while learning from the mechanics before driving west to Toormore. With this truck, Dad did weekly collections of butter and eggs from farmers all over the peninsula.

By the time I was born in 1949, my grandfather had just died, and the shop was the only business the family had left. The milling and produce collection had been wiped out by changes in the agricultural infrastructure. A large government-supported organization supplied both services to the exclusion of small operators.

Although as children we never felt we wanted for anything, we lived abstemiously, which is why Dad rarely gave gifts.

However, he took me to Skibbereen one day to get some messages and stopped on the street outside the jewelers. "Your mother needs a new watch," he said. We entered the shop, where he proceeded to buy a modest and sensible design. I never saw him before or after buy such an extravagant gift.

While Dad was not a great gift-giver, it was not easy to give him a gift either. Many years later, I brought him a pair of expensive binoculars from one of my overseas trips. I knew he liked to view birds and boats at sea. Apart from insisting I shouldn't have bought it for him, he made a point of showing me where he stored it on top of the sideboard in our dining room and said, "I will keep it safe for you there." And he did.

He had few pleasures that he demonstrated or spoke of, but he relished being out on the sea and he valued fishing in his small wooden boat. He showed me how to bait hooks, jag the line to ensure a new catch stayed hooked, and pull a mackerel's head backward to end its flapping. He also taught me how to moor the boat on an ingenious pulley system he had devised to keep it off the rocks when not in use. We rowed everywhere in the early days. Later, he bought a small two-and-a-half-horsepower Seagull outboard motor, which he valued and of which he took great care. I loved that boat too and the uninterrupted time with him. We did not communicate much by word or emotional exchange, but these were the best of times. The fresh salt smell of the sea, the raucous call of the gulls, the noise of the oars in the water, the lapping of water against the hull and, if we were lucky, the sun in our faces, made a perfect universe.

I think one of the reasons Dad enjoyed his boat was that he was free of Mom ordering and making rules. He was decidedly lacking in ambition, partly because there were no meaningful work options beyond laboring. He was a generation too soon to get free universal education, and engineering and science-based jobs, to which his talents were well suited, were non-existent. Mom probably resented his lack of drive, but at the same time, her being the driving force suited them both. Their relationship mellowed over the years to mutual acceptance rather than a romantic fairytale.

Dad reached his sixties when I was still in my teens. It was not uncommon at that time for men to be in their forties before getting married, partly as a result of a reluctance to leave their mothers, who spoiled them with plenty of bad habits. This made retraining an uphill task for the future wives.

When he refused to take the telephone, as the service was being offered in our region for the first time, I realized he was becoming frozen in time and resistant to most new gadgets. He found modern contraptions and habits difficult to accept.

In his later years, he complained about modern dancing habits, people's dress, and in short, anything that smacked of change. I butted heads with him about these attitudes, and it took me many years before I understood something of what he was going through. Little had changed in Toormore for over a hundred years, since the Famine in the mid-1800s, through his youth, and right up to the 1960s.

Then, in the space of about ten to twenty years, everything changed. He complained about the price of everyday things, where prices had remained stable for years. Dark, somber clothes, virtually unchanged in a century, were giving way to the psychedelic paraphernalia of the hippies. New bands and dancehalls replaced the outdoor dancing in the summer and at selected homes in the winter. A huge central animal market in Skibbereen, with formal auction procedures and men in white coats, wiped out the monthly community Fair Day in Goleen. The sleek, efficient Combined Harvester replaced the annual ritual of the threshing at every household. It accomplished its work efficiently without the need for a community.

He also missed the wakes. They were beginning to be replaced by new-fangled and misleadingly-named Funeral Parlours.

"We had great times at wakes, Bill," he told me. "When I was young, there was free booze and cigarettes for two days and nights, and it was a great place for storytelling."

5

MY MOTHER

My mother, Anne—called Nan—was born in 1918 in the Roycroft's original homestead. When she was a child, the family moved to Carrigmanus, a mile to the east. There were four brothers and four sisters; she was third from the end. By all accounts, she had an idyllic childhood on a farm that, compared to most neighbours, was relatively prosperous. The large number in the family made them very self-sufficient.

Her three sisters went off to nursing, including the two who were younger than her. She had finally decided to go too. One evening she went to the cow house to tell her father. She told me he looked up from milking a cow and said with tears in his eyes, "Nannie, who will we have to look after us if you go too?" She melted and couldn't work up the courage to go after that. Whether or not her indecision had anything to do with my father being in the picture at that stage is hard to know.

I know little about their courtship except that, like many men at the time, Dad (Tom) took at least ten years to make a move. At one stage, she corresponded with a sister to get advice as to what she should do. Another aunt told me they regularly met at the rectory gates in Goleen, he cycling the four miles from Toormore, and she the five miles from Carrigmanus.

There is only one sepia photograph of the wedding outside the church in Goleen; it is lit so badly you would not recognize the wedding party unless you knew who they were. They went for a week to Dublin for their honeymoon, which would have been regarded as an ambitious venture for the times, in 1945.

There was immediate trouble when Mom moved into Dad's home in Toormore. His mother, Bess, didn't get on with most people, not least her new daughter-in-law. She expected Mom to wait on her hand and foot and was never pleased. The next trauma was when Mom had her first child, a girl, who died after a few days in Schull Hospital. The facilities were frugal, and child mortality was still very high at that time. She never spoke about it but it was particularly sad in hindsight when she went on to have three boys but no girl.

Soon after this, Mom and Dad decided to take off to Bristol, where my mother had an uncle and aunt in a big house; they welcomed them to stay. They had no children of their own and it was understood they would leave the house to Mom and Dad eventually. My oldest brother, Rich, was born there. There is a lovely photograph of the grandparents from Carrigmanus who came all the way to Bristol for the Christening.

In this, and a few other photographs, Mom was a good-looking young woman—all five-feet-two inches of her. She had jet-black hair worn to the shoulders like most of the young women of her time. Her face had a Mediterranean influence like all the rest of her family. Instead of walking, she half ran, like there was an urgency about everywhere she had to go.

Mom and Dad were making a new life in Bristol when they got word that Dad's father, Dick, was on the way out. They left most of their belongings behind as they made haste back to Ireland on the assumption that it would be a short stay. Mom was heavily pregnant with me at that stage and she went straight to Carrigmanus to stay with her mother. It was a difficult time for her, and giving birth to me must have further constrained her options. Dick's demise and death took several months. Mom moved back in at Toormore, and for whatever reasons, she and Dad decided to put off a return to England, and eventually did not go back to Bristol. That is how close I was to being brought up as an Englishman. It was a decision I know she regretted more than once. She had been very happy there, free from the expectations of her mother-in-law; I think she also enjoyed the city life, as rural life in Ireland at that time was very constricting. A compromise solution to living with Bess was reached when we moved across the road to a small house, called the cottage, that had been owned by the family for years. It consisted of two rooms downstairs and two upstairs and a lean-to at the back for washing and toilet.

From my earliest memories, I always knew my mother loved me, as she did my brothers, without favourites. She was warm but not demonstrative in a physical way; there were few hugs. While city dwellers were more into embraces and cuddles, most rural people did not demonstrate their love physically for their spouse or children. One of the reasons for this could be farmers' wives having an abundance of children, making physical intimacy a chore. Another could be the heavy blanket of religion that tended to view all physical expression with suspicion. My mother was proud of her three boys and dressed us coordinately when in public; she ensured cleanliness by the weekly wash every Saturday evening where she soaked us in turn in a large metal bath in the kitchen.

My second brother, David, was born in the cottage, and sometime after that, we moved back into the main house again. Bess was going downhill and there was pressure on Mom to take care of her. This again must have been a very difficult time for her, as she also began to take over running the shop. Coming from a thriving farm, she had been led to believe that the Jermyns were well-off, but she slowly found out that most of the wealth amassed by Dick had been dissipated, partly spent by Bess, and they were now in a perilous position.

Despite their best efforts, they were not able to make ends meet and the fifties in Ireland was not a place that offered many job opportunities. Dad headed off to Birmingham with a friend who got him a job driving a delivery van with a company that made electric heaters. When he returned home for a Christmas visit, he brought me a fancy wooden pencil case for my school bag. It was long and narrow with different compartments and a sliding cover. I was so proud, showing it to my schoolmates.

When he left to return to Birmingham in the New Year, Mom sat crying gently at the top of the stairs. I wondered what was wrong, not comprehending, apart from missing Dad, she now had the responsibility of running the store as well as bringing up three young children all by herself. After about two years, Dad finally returned and stayed at home, and somehow after that, they were able to make the economics work, at least from a child's eyes.

A huge step for her was learning to drive after we had grown up as it increased her independence and opened up a whole new world. She took to driving, like all her activities, fearlessly and with total commitment. In her later years, when she probably should not have been driving, she tended to hog the middle of the road and drive faster than she realized. A friend told me, "Bill, it is okay for us locals—we know her and keep out of her way, but I am worried about German or French tourists in the summer."

Because Mom and Dad had only primary education, it was difficult for them to give me any career guidance, and discussion on current affairs and politics was also difficult, in particular when I was in my teens and thought I knew everything. When I was whining to Mom once that I would never figure out what I wanted to do, I received good advice: "Well, at least you will find out what you don't want to do," she said, as she finished washing some clothes.

One incident in particular illustrates her ongoing development through life and made me proud of her. I was visiting with my family and some of their friends. They were joking about and someone made a disparaging comment about gays. Mom, who would never have even heard of gays in her youth and later listened to a lot of prejudice against them, piped up, "Aren't they all God's children?"

In her marriage, Mom was the boss. She was a natural take-charge type and Dad was of an easygoing style; for the most part this situation suited him. Now and again, he would erupt and there could be days of silence between them. However, after reconciliation, she always remained the boss. While there was no visible intimacy between them, or with us children, I think they had a reasonable marriage. They were both pragmatic about making the marriage work. In the forties and fifties, expectations of marriage were modest compared to today's values. Women, in particular, were seen as little more than baby-making machines. Against that background, they had a good marriage.

6

WILLIAMSONS

Dick, Ben, and Jane Williamson were an integral part of my life growing up. Bess, my paternal grandmother, was their aunt, and they were like surrogate grandparents to us children. Their house was close behind ours; I reached it by running up the pathway past the outhouse, past the henhouse, and then down the slope into their backyard. Their parents originally lived at the back of the yard in a small house that was now used for storage; the open fireplace was still in place. My grandfather built their present house in 1913. I know the date because it was inscribed on one of the chimneys.

None of them married and the three continued to live together after their parents and an older brother died. Dick was the oldest and the most easygoing and good-natured. He may have had a slight mental disability as he was childlike in many of his utterances and tended to do what he was told by the other two. He'd had all his teeth extracted but never bothered to get dentures and so his lips and cheeks were sunken in a half-moon face. Jane would typically cut his food into small pieces. One day, in the middle of their lunch, a visiting neighbour told me Dick asked Ben to borrow his dentures for a piece of meat that had defeated him. Ben reluctantly removed them and passed them over. Dick quickly bore down on the offending piece of meat, extracted the dentures, and returned them to Ben.

After lunch, Dick stretched out on the long seat between the table and the front window for his daily siesta. He had never travelled further than twenty miles from home, and that was to the nearest large town of Skibbereen. He was content.

Ben had a pleasant face and wore glasses and a hat. He walked with a limp because of some unexplained accident. While he was not a regular drinker, when he headed to Schull on rare occasions in his horse and cart, he tended to get scuttered. One evening, a friend was in the yard talking to Jane when Ben came home flat-out in the cart while the horse navigated her way. Jane jawed him up and down but he did not respond while he struggled to unharness the horse and then staggered into the house. He shared power with Jane, but not willingly. Whenever she felt the need to fight for her rights, there was only one winner.

Jane was an extremely good-looking woman with long, flowing, white hair when she let it down. A long time afterwards I heard she had been dating a local man but this broke up in acrimony. The families were involved and I surmise that mixed religion was a key issue.

Jane was the main point of contact for Rich and me because she was always at home while the men were out working the farm. Sometimes we spent more time with her than in our own house. She fussed over us, and like a grandparent, gave us goodies that our mother would not. When electricity came to Toormore for the first time, in a case of play imitating life, I took to the trees behind Jane's house with Rich and our friends, Andy and Richie, to play at erecting poles and wires.

We used waste explosive wire from the electric workers to string between the trees as simulated electric cable. Jane would appear regularly and warn us of the danger of falling, which, of course, we ignored. Another time I fell into a dirty pool of water and destroyed my pants. I was terrified of owning up to my mother. Jane took me into her kitchen, took my pants and washed them, and then dried them in front of the fire.

Williamsons's was the centre for the dentist's visits. The dentist visited once a month. He set up in front of the fire, and his main offering was extractions. There were many young people I knew who felt it was cool to have all their teeth out by the age of eighteen. I was scheduled one day because of ongoing pain in a tooth and ordered to be home in good time from school to catch the dentist before his departure. I was afraid and dilly-dallied on my bicycle on the way. I got a bollocking from my mother for keeping the dentist waiting, and this probably had not helped his mood either. In no time, he froze my gums and started pulling. Despite the numbing, the pain was excruciating and when he yanked the tooth out, there was material stuck to the roots, which I later found out was called an abscess.

The Williamsons kept pigs and needed them slaughtered periodically. Johnny Kingston, the grave digger, killed a pig for them once a year. I was there once when he did the deed. The biggest pig was isolated and pulled from the others, and then subdued and turned on its back. Johnny slit its throat with one deft cut of his special hooked knife. The pig was held down until its life ebbed away with the flowing blood. A crowbar was inserted through the joints of the hind legs of the dead pig and it was hoisted by a rope strung over the horizontal branch of a tree. I felt a little sorry for the pig, but otherwise was unaffected.

Johnny then lit up his blowlamp and proceeded to burn off all the hair from the carcass of the hanging pig. When this was completed, he lowered the pig again and began the job of cleaning out the entrails and carving the pig into a variety of cuts. Jane sent us kids around Toormore with a cut of meat for every neighbour, and apart from some kept for current consumption, she salted the rest away for the year ahead. This was done by placing the cuts in a large wooden barrel between layers of salt. My mother roasted the cut we received. I particularly loved the roasted skin, referred to as crackling, for its taste and crunchiness. The taste and aroma of roast pork have stayed with me through the years and it has always been one of my favourite foods.

Their house was also the main place for *scoraiochting* (storytelling) in Toormore. This old pursuit involved storytelling, gossip, and any other entertainment introduced by those who attended. Several nights of the week, neighbours sampled the joys of the evening. Dick would be set up on the sofa by the window. Eugene Sullivan could be at one side of the stove. He had a great sense of humour and was a man of mystery to us children. He had been the postman in his younger day and logged many miles walking up and down our peninsula.

Pats Coughlan would usually be ensconced at the other side of the stove, smoking his pipe. The stove was of special interest to me, with little doors at each side, as well as at the front. I would usually sit beside Pats, mainly quiet, as children were expected to be then, drinking in the atmosphere and conversation. Pats was a small man who lived on his own in a very small house, the front door of which he never opened to God or man. He also had all the news and seemed to be privy to every bit of gossip going.

One evening, Pats showed me some tricks, one of which I can still do. It involved making a "True Lover's Knot" from a sheet of paper and required many folds before emerging with a complex and pleasant-looking knot. It was impossible to pull apart without knowing the secret of how to pull in the right places—maybe an apt metaphor for the real thing.

7

MIKE BUTLER

Mike Butler was one of the last reminders of my grandmother's high life, where she was used to having a number of servants. He was a small well-built man who wore a hat and chewed tobacco whenever he could get it, which he spat out of the side of his mouth with accuracy and elegance.

Mike lived with us when I was a child; my brothers and I adored him as he was always good to us and gave us a lot of attention. He was a man of mystery; all we knew about him was that he was born in the region and had gone to America. When he came home, he had no family left, and somehow, he came into the employ of my grandmother and moved into the house, where he acted effectively as her personal servant. When she died, as he had nowhere to go, he remained on as part of the household. His tenure under my mother was relatively harmonious except for now and again she would catch him sneaking a plug of tobacco out of the shop to feed his tobacco-chewing habit, and there would be ructions. We tended to be on Mike's side, as he was normally so good-natured, we didn't like to see him get into trouble. This habit, and his food, were his only expenses on the house.

In addition to servicing Bess' needs, before my time, Mike accompanied my father in the truck when they collected butter and eggs from the region. He told me once about the few cheaters who would put water or a stone in the middle of their butter to increase the weight. Obviously, he and my father must have left a positive effect on the community, because years later, when I did extra postman duty at Christmas, if the families learned who I was, I received a very strong welcome. I had to go into each house for tea, and sometimes liquor.

One morning, Mike had breakfast with me and headed out to watch some men who were working on the laneway a behind the house. A short time later, one of the men came running into the kitchen to say Mike had had a "bad turn." I ran to the corner of the lane where the men were working to see Mike stretched out on the ground. My father appeared. "Get down to the post office and ask Teddy to ring the doctor and the priest," he said. I cycled down the hill to the post office at top speed.

When I returned, I realized Mike was dead. The man and my father had taken an old door from the mill storage room and transported him back to "lie in state" in the mill room. Mike hadn't caused trouble to anyone during his life, and the same was true for his death. He was buried nearby in an ancient graveyard, Cill hAngill—Church of the Angels—dating from the Middle Ages. The graveyard has since gone into disuse and is grown over; it would be difficult for anyone to find him now. I doubt there is any recorded reference to the life he lived, save for this mention. This is a meagre tribute to a life well lived.

8

SCHOOL

Mr. Powell drove Rich and me to the nearest Protestant elementary school every day. He was our local cleric, and the only person for miles with a car, a Volkswagen Beetle with split back and front windows and indicators that flipped outwards like small wings from behind the doors.

I liked the small one-roomed school. It had about a dozen students spread across the grades from ages four to fourteen. Our teacher, Mrs. Hunt, was a rotund lady, extremely patient and very skilled at managing all of us. One day, a boy stuck a paper tail in a small hole in her skirt at the top of her ample posterior. She didn't feel a thing. For the next hour we were all in paroxysms of laughter as the tail wagged while she flounced around the room. She was good-natured about it when she discovered the cause of our mirth. I liked Mrs. Hunt and that school. She had a great way with children.

When I was five, Rich and I switched to another one-room schoolhouse about four miles away from Toormore near the closest village, Goleen. We moved because our mode of transport, Mr. Powell, retired, and we were able to travel to and from the new school by the daily mail van that also carried passengers. This school introduced a total new freedom. The official playground was as small as a postage stamp, so the teacher, Miss O'Neill, allowed us to play along the narrow by-road from Helen's garage in the north to the four-arched bridge just before entering Goleen in the south. One of our games was chariot racing along this road, with the bigger children hauling chariots cut from large gorse bushes, while I, as one of the smaller ones, rode on the bushes. I was friendly with one of the stronger boys, who made me his charioteer; I liked to win and we did often.

Another of our favourite pursuits was seesawing on the chassis of an old hearse that had been abandoned by Helen's garage. We maneuvered the chassis onto a ledge at the side of the road such that it could lift and drop around a hard rock. We perched in groups on each end. There were many falls and injuries. I have a scar on the side of my forehead where I fell and hit a rock.

At least half of us were related, coming from a small Protestant community. I had five Roycroft first cousins, for example. Another cousin and I were working together with math exercises and the teacher gave us permission to proceed at our own pace. My cousin and I agreed to do ten or so questions each evening. When I discovered that she had raced ahead, passing our agreed target by a significant amount, I was outraged. When I got home, I told my mother. "Catch up and discuss it with her so you are not embarrassed with the teacher again," she said. I sat at the kitchen table for hours, until I finished the whole book.

One of the great things about one-room schools was the way each student could progress at his or her own pace with the seniors expected to help the juniors. A particular girl was older than me but much further behind everyone in her ability. She had protruding eyes and puffy lips, didn't talk very well, and found it difficult to do more than the most basic arithmetic. Everyone said she was "a bit foolish." She was also deaf, so the teacher taught us all the basic ten-fingered sign language, which I still remember today. We didn't make a fuss over her and incorporated her as best as possible in our games.

Her brother was a gentle giant but not gifted academically. One day, the regional inspector planned a visit. Miss O'Neill had coached us for days and tried to engineer things such that the boy would not be singled out for questions. As luck would have it, the first person selected by the inspector was the boy. "What's your name, boy?" asked the inspector.

"Johnny," answered the boy.

"Come up to the map here," ordered the inspector, "and show me the county

Galway."

Johnny shuffled up to the map, which was standing on a big easel, took the pointer offered by the inspector, and started to stab all over the surface like a drunken sailor.

"Ok, boy," said the inspector. "Galway is in the middle of the country and a long way from you here, so I don't expect you to know where to find it. Show me Kerry instead."

Kerry is right beside Cork in the very southwest but now Johnny crawled the pointer up to Donegal on the northwest of the country. Miss O'Neill was red in the face, powerless, as all her good work to impress the inspector went slowly down the drain.

9
THRESHING

The annual "thrashing," as the threshing was called, was a rite-of-passage in the fall and a high point of community cooperation and socialization. I always looked forward to Babe Donovan's threshing in the barnyard across the road from her house. Babe had two large fields growing oats; the cutting was done about two weeks in advance of the threshing, and the men leaned the sheaves together in fours and fives to form stooks (standing groups). When these had dried, they were brought to the haggard (barnyard) with several trips of horse and cart. The sheaves were built on each other to form a large stack at one side of where the threshing machine would be stationed. When the first stack was built to about twelve feet, another stack was built opposite the first so that there was room for the thresher in between.

The long-awaited thresher rarely arrived on time because it depended on how much oats was in the previous haggard. Eventually, it came up the road slowly, towed by the owner on his tractor. The men of Toormore followed. They traditionally worked together at each farm until all the oats in the parish were threshed. The thresher needed quite an amount of 'nurturing' to get through the narrow gates of the barnyard. Part of the challenge in the region was getting the thresher in and out of the small haggards (yards). The gates were not made for such a large machine. Eventually the thresher squeezed in and was then reversed between the two stacks.

The owner connected the tractor to the thresher using a belt and two flywheels. The beast was now ready to spring to action, drawing life from the tractor. Up close, the thresher looked like a Tyrannosaurus rex, with a large mouth at one end and exhaust-like chutes at the other. Two men climbed up on the first stack and two more climbed on top of the machine. The men on the stacks threw the sheaves to the men on the machine. They ripped off the binding and fed the sheaves to the voracious jaws of the hopper.

Across the road, in Babe's kitchen, I smelled the sweet aroma of bacon boiling in the large pot on the turf-burning stove, and the even more beguiling scent of cabbage. Neighbourhood women were there assisting with the food preparation for a meal when the threshing was done. I heard the gurgling sound of the permanently boiling tureen of water, ready to sate the constant requirement for fresh tea. I shuttled across the road, with buckets half-filled with milky tea and lumps of bread, while the other kids ferried bottles of black porter. Work stopped as the men lay on the straw on the stacks and on the thresher to drink their porter or tea.

The thresher seemed to grow taller as the flanking stacks of oats grew smaller, while its inner workings were mysterious due to the amazing exterior array of wheels and belts that whirred and strafed with hypnotic regularity. The vibrating baffles issued their familiar ululating roar. The oats were digested into the bowels of the machine, and it began to spit the separated straw out of the front end, like some regurgitating prehistoric beast. On the ground at the back of the thresher, I helped with the bags that were slowly filling with the warm grain. There were four outlet chutes with jute bags attached to each. My job was to watch out for bags filling and close off the shutter on the chute. When the men took away the bag, I attached an empty bag and opened the chute again. I was six years old.

Under the overall high-pitched roar of the machine were the individual sounds of some of the hard-working parts, the whirring of a wheel, the slapping of a belt, and the clapping of the baffles: whirr, whirr, awhirr, slap, slap, whirr, whirr, awhirr, clap, clap, whirr, whirr awhirr … all combined to create a friendly symphony of sound. The machine weaved its magic with the community in harmony, nothing in order, but everything in its place.

10

STATIONS

My mother was often chosen to be one of the chief caterers at the breakfast after the "stations." She knew how to do things properly, and the Catholic neighbours were comfortable with her, as she, albeit a Protestant, was well trusted over the years. The "stations" referred to the Stations of the Cross and a Catholic Mass that was performed in a different home every spring. The particular family chosen would be expected to paint up the inside and whitewash the outside of the house, in respect for the revered figure of the priest. The event was greeted with mixed feelings—the effort involved in cleaning and preparing was immense, but it meant each house was smartened up at least once every ten years.

My mother used to take me with her, and this time we were at a nearby house. A large black stove dominated the room at the end on the left, with chairs at each side. A long table stretched down the near side under the window. The room served as kitchen, dining, and sitting room. At the right end there was a door into the parlour. This was the official dining room but was only used during the year when a cat went in to sleep on a chair, or an errant hen came in the front door and picked its way around the bric-a-brac of accumulated years.

It had been scrupulously cleaned for the big event and augmented by my mother with a few added props of respectability. She had put a mat inside the door and coloured throw rugs to cover the battered chairs. This was where the priest would be served breakfast after the mass was celebrated.

Accustomed as she was to catering for clerics of her own religion, my mother knew how to set the table for the priest. She devised what she thought was a suitable menu for a man of his status. She was familiar with new delicacies like Kellogg's Cornflakes, and she put a little knitted cozy over the priest's boiled egg, fussed around, and generally made him feel important. Someone also had to have breakfast with the priest, so the man of the house, the local intellectual, was delegated this important role. As soon as the priest finished breakfast, he accepted a bag of potatoes and a bag of cabbage from the neighbour, and thoughtfully disappeared, leaving the natives to start an all-day party.

11

ALTAR CHURCH

This Church of Ireland (Anglican) church is unique in Ireland; it was built during the Great Famine, in the late 1840s, by a charismatic cleric, Fischer, who spoke Irish fluently, and gave it the official Irish name of "Teampaill na mBocht" ("Church of the Poor.")

We attended every Sunday as the main ritual of the week. Rich and I sat in a pew near the front under the supervision of Miss Johnson, one of the last of the Anglo Irish in our region, as my mother played the organ. She began to play the organ in the 1950s. Years previously, in her teens, the clergyman's wife picked on her to be her successor playing the organ and taught her to play. This was the beginning of over sixty years playing in three different churches, sometimes all on the same Sunday. She was not actually very accomplished, but what she lacked in technique she made up for with enthusiasm. Whenever she hit a wrong note, which was not infrequently, she would continue playing until she found the right one, then hit it with triumphant force. I had to endure her practicing every Saturday night on her piano at home. In addition to the wrong note procedure, she felt the same freedom to strike chords consecutively until she was satisfied that she had struck the right one.

My father sat at the back with many of the unconvinced. At a certain age, Rich and I gravitated to the back seat, opposite the font, to join our father. At a later time, a friend and I carved our initials on the edge of the bookshelf on this last pew—Easter '69. It remains there to this day.

The church is small, austere, and unpretentious, with no trappings of grandeur. Until recently, the bell over the porch was suspended from an old Volkswagen car chassis that had been erected by my grandfather. The walls are mercifully nearly completely free of memorial plaques to esteemed citizens. No recognition here to brigadiers or colonels who served the empire in India or Africa and remembered in many other Church of Ireland churches with large and ornate wall plaques. Our poor area didn't produce this kind of leader, and the ordinary folk would not have had the resources for such vanity.

Save for a large memorial to Fisher near the front, the only intrusion on the south wall is a small, simple white plaque to the four young men from Toormore—Cunningham, Wright, and two Donovan brothers—who lost their lives in the first World War. My father told me that their mother, who lived down the road, got word about her sons' deaths within a week of each other. It is as if the community felt this was the only tragedy between the Famine and the present time that merited commemoration.

There was a strong Church of Ireland population in the area at the time of the Famine, but Fisher was motivated to give work and food to all the impoverished and hungry locals while building the church. Soup was the main source of remuneration for this work and so the derogatory phrases "Souper" and "Taking the Soup" were used by some because many Catholics changed religion and joined Fischer in the new Anglican church. It is a matter of conjecture whether he was motivated primarily by human compassion or by missionary zeal. Without question, he did a lot of good for the community. Records exist of letters he wrote to London seeking money and food; he also introduced flax growing to the area. My great-grandmother worked at some stage in his rectory.

A few years later, the Catholic bishop of Cork decided to mount a "counter reformation" at the Altar. To lead this effort he recruited his nephew, a Corkman, who worked with the Hudson Bay Company in the wilds of Canada, and who was proficient in "taming" the natives. He was reputed to sit on a big horse outside the church door on Sundays and whip recalcitrant Catholic churchgoers. We don't know how this finished up, but the Anglican church and community thrived.

My observation more than 100 years later was that the few descendants of "Souper" families were convenience members of the church. In general, they would use the church for baptism and burial, and maybe Christmas. And many of them married Catholics and crossed back again. The "Soupers" were pragmatic about when to take the soup, hot, lukewarm, or cold. After that active and controversial start, the Church of Ireland (Anglican) community settled back into a fairly anonymous and peaceful existence.

Our family grave is on the north side, near the front door, and so far in my time, seven have been buried there. It must be one of the few churches in Ireland where you can look out over the sea—as peaceful a spot as you could choose for final resting. It often comforted me to know, as I passed the grave each Sunday, that while I was uncertain where I was going in life, I could be sure where I would end up.

12

FIRST VACATION

Rich and I went to Belfast one summer, to visit my uncle's family. I was six years old and Rich was seven.

We travelled by train from Cork to Dublin, where we stayed with friends before completing the trip to Belfast. The flat countryside with large fields I could see from the train was an eye opener for me coming from the rocky hills and mountains and small fields of West Cork.

My uncle, a Church of Ireland clergyman, his wife, and three kids were living in a beautiful red brick house between Malone and Lisburn roads—the centre of upper middle-class respectability.

My aunt Mary took me upstairs to show me the bathroom, a lovely Victorian bathroom where she pointed out the hot and the cold taps on the huge washbasin. Later, I went to use the bathroom but got only cold water from both taps. I shyly pointed this out to my aunt, and she started laughing as she escorted me back to the bathroom. She showed me how to leave the hot tap running for some time before it became hot. I was mortified, and even more so when I overheard her telling some of her coffee-morning friends about the incident the next day.

We spent many happy hours playing with our cousins in the secluded back garden. There was a garden shed in the centre and it had a circular rail on which it could rotate. We would divide into teams and push against each other in an effort to rotate the shed in one direction or the other. Sometimes my uncle would push against all of us, until he strained his back one day.

One afternoon, we were playing soccer in the back garden. A high wall separated us from the neighbours, and of course, inevitably, the ball sailed over. We had been warned not to go next door, but I could see no harm in retrieving the ball and did so anyway. When my aunt heard the story, she explained to me that the neighbours were Catholic. I could not understand at the time what the problem was. It was my first exposure to the fact that all may not be well between the religions in Ireland, especially in Belfast.

My first ride in a double-decker bus was magical. Rich and I were up at the front windows on the top as the bus cruised along Malone Road to the centre of Belfast. I couldn't have wished for anything better in the world. The buses were red and much more exciting than the green buses in the South. The mixture of large redbrick houses and magnificent official-looking limestone buildings indicated great wealth in this city.

13
TURNING POINT

I was ten years old when I began my exit from West Cork. This was the 'road less travelled' at the time; I had a visceral reaction against taking it and did not like where I thought it would lead me. My mother had decided that her children were going to get a decent education. At that time, nobody in our area went beyond elementary school, and the nearest secondary school was twenty miles away. However, it was a Catholic school and, being Protestant, she was not going to send us there.

She transferred Rich and me from our second elementary school back to the first one, because the teacher would not give us special tuition for the scholarship exam to one of the nearest Protestant secondary schools, Midleton College. It was ninety miles away, near Cork city, which, without a car, may as well have been the southern tip of Yemen. There was another, closer school, Bandon Grammar, but our local cleric had been a student at Midleton many years earlier, so he was a strong influence on the process. Simultaneously, my mother organized the purchase of an old caravan, set it up for rent on the beach near our home, and became the first holiday renter in the area. Her idea was that the income would go towards the cost of our education.

When the time for the scholarship exam arrived, my mother delegated my father to take Rich and me to Midleton. We set off by the evening bus to Cork city, where we stayed on the outskirts overnight at my aunt Sadie's farm. She gave us a ride to the bus to Midleton in the early morning. I clearly remember my first sight of the College—an imposing gateway with a huge round stone ball on each pillar, a gate lodge on the left, and the main building an imposing presence at the top of a long rising driveway. Years later I decided it looked like a cross between a reform school and a prison.

The exam was held in one of the main classrooms. Everything seemed so big. Rich and I were placed up near the front. Most of the boys wore short, grey pants to the mid-thigh, while a few wore long pants. Rich and I wore short corduroy pants down to our knees. Some of the kids were older, some seemed to be already in the school, and all spoke with a variety of strange accents. The boy beside me had what I knew to be a yo-yo, and a swanky keychain ran from his belt to his pocket.

The headmaster, a big blustery man with large eyebrows wearing a black flowing gown, came in just before 9:00 a.m. to start the exam. He handed out the first tests and told us to start. Rich put his hand up to say we had no ink. Looking around, I realized all the others had either ballpoint or fountain pens, while Rich and I had only basic dip pens. It wasn't that we were that poor, it was simply because our teacher back in the elementary school would not let us use the other pens, in case they would ruin our handwriting.

Much to the entertainment of all present, the headmaster rummaged around in a large cupboard and eventually came up with two inkwells and ink for the two hillbillies. We finally got going at 9:10 a.m. I was red in the face and wanted to quit. But I didn't. I was very competitive at that age and able to focus totally on an objective. I didn't want to disappoint my mother.

A few weeks later, I came home from school one day to be ushered into the sitting room by my mother, and where the local cleric waited. They announced that I had got first place in the scholarship exam, and Rich was third. I took this news in stride because I still did not understand the full implications. Although I was not yet eleven, my childhood was over, and I would be leaving home and going into a culture I did not choose. Once immersed, there would be no way back.

Late that summer my mother purchased new suitcases and the basic prescribed clothing. The night before departure date, the enormity of what was happening finally hit and I spent several hours crying by the fire. Next day, Rich and I got a ride from the father of a boy who was already a student and lived in Skibbereen. To get there, we got a ride from a friend with Mom and Dad standing waving outside the shop until we went out of sight at the corner. My mother cried while Dad took his usual stoical mode. Looking out the back window with tears in my eyes was a scene repeated many times in the future. I was always prone to car-sickness and with the extra stress I suffered the embarrassment of having to call for a stop on several occasions on the trip from Skibbereen to Midleton.

On arrival, Rich and I were allocated to the smallest dormitory—just three beds—directly over the imposing front door and close to the headmaster's quarters. He was also from West Cork, and he and his wife took a special interest in our welfare. She visited to 'tuck us in' on the first night and for many nights thereafter to make us feel at home. While I appreciated her gesture, she had no children of her own, she was not my mother, and this was far from home.

We went downstairs to a huge dining room in the morning. I sat in the middle of a long table facing one wall. Tears flowed down my face into my porridge. My abject loneliness in this alien environment exceeded the embarrassment of worrying who, if anyone, saw me. This performance continued on and off for weeks, and also spontaneously at unexpected times. I thought I would never see home again.

I suffered horribly from homesickness and also felt like an outsider compared to the majority of boys who were primarily from the middle-class of Cork city. As well as our different style of short pants, we also had different 'country' accents and started off by using dip pens. I would spend most of the night prior to returning for the next term crying. I used to beg my mother to allow me stay at home.

Rich didn't outwardly show the same pain at leaving home and family. He was more than a year older, and also, I think his temperament was more suited to handling change. My sense of alienation was compounded by some students, and one teacher mocking my strong West Cork accent on a regular basis. My mode of dress was also a subject of ridicule.

At ten, I was the youngest at the school. My mother had sent me as company for my brother, but she didn't realize the traumatic effect it would have. Without realizing the pain it must have caused her, I used to beg her to allow me to stay at home. She wanted to give us a decent education and future; that was not important to me then. All I wanted was to stay close to home.

The trauma paid an unexpected visit recently when I asked my neighbour what age was her son, as he was celebrating a birthday. "Ten," she said. I reeled in shock as he still appeared to me as a small child.

"At that age, I was sent away to boarding school," I responded, and it was her turn to be shocked. It brought home to me in a way I had not considered before, I was a child ill-suited to immersion into an intellectually limiting middle-class urban environment and regimented lifestyle. Later in life, I resented the religious and political forces that allowed a childhood to be stolen in this manner. The larger issues at play were the government's lack of interest in the educational facilities for rural Protestants and the decidedly un-Christian attitudes of both Protestants and Catholics to each other's welfare.

My experience was that it may have suited those who were in the mainstream. However, for the few who were different, their life was generally made very unpleasant. By different, I included those who were artistically or musically inclined, those who were not interested in sport, and those who were uncertain about their sexuality. Mercifully, I ticked none of these boxes.

Over time, I was broken into the system. I had some good teachers who influenced me positively. Maths was my favourite subject, probably because I related to the teacher, who worked collaboratively and never dictated. The history and English teacher was eccentric, entertaining and stimulating. He encouraged us to think for ourselves in both subjects. To him, I owe my lifelong interest in English and history and the development of my "Outsider" personality, where I began to feel comfortable being a contrarian and having different views to the mainstream on religion and politics.

The science teacher had moved from industry to teaching and was authentic without any of the aura surrounding some of the others. He freely admitted to not being too clever and he instilled in us the quality of hard work. We had only one female teacher for Irish and French, whom I liked. She was very quiet and shy, but firm. She had very pale skin that frequently reddened with embarrassment in a wide variety of situations.

One day I, and many of the others, were embarrassed and amused in turn. The boy who sat beside me was always fiddling and she used to castigate him regularly for this. This day she was sitting on top of the unoccupied desk in front of him with her feet on the seat. He had his book resting between his desk and his lap and seemed to be fiddling underneath. "What are you doing down there?" she said to the boy as she reached down to put a stop to his distraction. She grabbed the book, exposing the boy masturbating. She jumped up, reddened, and ran out of the classroom. Later the male 'chief enforcer' teacher arrived and meted out detention and other punishments to all.

This situation possibly arose because in our previous class our Latin teacher encouraged masturbation. I, and a few others, were too young to perform but got a good grounding for the future. He was a pervert, but benign in the sense of not molesting anyone, and sadly, he committed suicide a number of years later.

Once you take a child out of his environs and indoctrinate him in another culture, he cannot easily return. I make the analogy to the Canadian Indigenous Residential Schools, without in any way suggesting my case was close to the horrors inflicted on the Natives. However, looking back from adulthood, I realize my childhood being cut short caused me great trauma, limited the close emotional bond with my parents, influenced the direction of my life, and caused a sense of abandonment that surfaces from time to time to the present day. I don't blame my mother; she was only doing her best for us.

14

DAVID

When I was three years old, my younger brother David was born in the small house we lived in at the time in Toormore, across the road from the main Jermyn homestay. One night I heard crying from my parent's bedroom. The next morning, I was presented with the new addition to the family. I never felt curious how he came to be, or was crying in my parent's bedroom.

As he grew up, we realized he had a shortage of breath after a little exercise and his face turned purple. Rich, our friends, and I took this in our stride. We would have him participate in our games for as long as he could; he would then sit on his haunches to the side and watch. He never complained. On summer days my mother would carry him on her back on the steep path up from Barley Cove beach.

At home, I played with him most because I was closer in age to him than to Rich. We abused Spot, our long-suffering dog, by trying to ride him around the house and garden. We fought a lot because we were both very competitive, but there was no lasting rancor; instead, we had a strong feeling of family identity and bond. David had sallow skin and dark hair and was better looking than Rich and me. He topped his class in school. My mother sent him to the local Catholic school because it was within walking distance.

At some point, my mother was told by a doctor David had a blocked valve and a hole in the heart. The hole wasn't as serious, apparently, as the blocked valve, which was the cause of his lack of wind. She was advised that if he did not have surgery for the valve, he would probably live no longer than twenty.

I don't know how long she wrestled with this decision or discussed it with my father and David. The Williamsons were against the surgery, influenced presumably by the death of my father's sister after surgery many years before. I think David made the decision easier by saying he wanted to go for the operation. He was smart and mature beyond his years and wanted the opportunity to participate in normal activities. He was eleven years old.

At the appointed time he and my mother travelled to Cork and he checked into Sarsfield Court Hospital, which was relatively new at the time as it had been built as part of a scheme to eradicate TB. Then, after a few days, a nurses' strike was announced, and all surgeries were cancelled. Having psyched themselves up, they had to turn around and go home again. This must have been excruciating. Was this a sign? The cousins said it was.

Rich and I were boarding at Midleton College through all of this and the main means of communication was a weekly letter home. We were not involved in the detail and were fairly occupied in the bubble of school activity. Sometime later, my mother and David ventured to Cork for the second time.

The Sunday before the operation, Rich and I obtained permission from the school to visit our brother at Sarsfield Court.

All I remember of the visit was when we left, we had to descend an open stairwell that turned around and around in a square shape. David stood at the top with sad eyes, and he stayed there watching us until we reached the bottom and went out of sight.

Later that week, one evening when we were doing homework, the headmaster sent a message for Rich and me to come to his study. I was expecting a good progress report. Instead, he broke the news that David had died. I was numb with the shock and did not want to accept the message. I didn't have an emotional reaction until later when the reality sunk in.

Soon after, my mother arrived with two Cork friends who had kindly agreed to drive her. She told us the blocked valve had been fixed, but afterwards, his kidneys hadn't returned to function. There was no kidney machine there at that time. In the few days it took the lack of kidney function to take its toll, he had tubes all over but he was able to communicate with my mother by writing notes, and telling her he was ok.

She later told us she spent two days waiting for Maurice Hickey, the surgeon, to find out what had happened. When he finally deigned to see her, he gave little explanation, reasons, or solace. Anytime I revisited this memory I was glad in one sense I wasn't older as I would have gone in there and demanded a few answers and let him know he couldn't treat my mother with such lack of respect. It was entirely possible in those days they made an error. We'll never know now and I'm not sure it would've made a difference if we'd known then.

On a beautiful sunny day in May a few cousins, Rich and I took a slow walk from the hospital up the avenue to the small morgue. The foliage was lush with clumps of my beloved purple and red fuchsia offering respect from each side. Bees were buzzing between the blooms extracting the sweet nectar, like David and I often did as children at home by breaking off the flowers and sucking in the sweet liquid from the stem. The birds didn't interrupt their singing. Life went on.

Looking at David in the coffin helped me finally recognize he was dead. He was back to looking purple and one of his front teeth was exposed and was slightly crossed on the other. He was far, far away. We followed the hearse, a shining new black converted Cortina, in a convoy of cars on the long journey to the Altar Church in Toormore. At one stage, the hearse stopped for gas, and, as we waited behind, it seemed incongruous that it had to stop for something as mundane as gas. I had imagined a hearse being beyond worldly needs. We had a funeral service in the Altar church and buried him in the family grave.

Back at school I immersed myself in all the activity again. Now fourteen, I was self-centred and not very attentive to, and supportive of, my mother. Then again, communication was limited between school and home. When I came home for the summer vacation, seeing his bedroom empty but with all his toys and possessions undisturbed, was very upsetting. The realization that I would never see David again hit hard. There would be nobody to tell all the goings-on at school and nobody to play with the toys.

I didn't notice at first my mother's grieving. I did notice she lacked her usual spirit. I realized that with us away in school, she had had a few years of David's company and they both gained a lot out of it. Now she had a premature "empty nest." Her religious faith was very important to her, but in this case, it didn't seem to lift the clouds. The following summer, she still grieved and we worried about what we could do.

Then a message came that started her renewal. A friend told her that her mother-in-law attended Spiritualist séances in London and was given a message for a woman her daughter-in-law knew. The message was from the woman's son, David, and he told her to stop grieving, he was very happy. This was all my mother needed to start her on the road back, although there was a part of her died with him.

David was an exceptional guy with a great brain and courage to match. In the Altar Church behind the communion table, there is a plain wooden cross to his memory, made by the rector at the time. There was a photograph of him looking beatific on the steps of the church chancel in a place of pride on the dresser in the home dining room. There was another framed photograph of us three brothers all dressed in the same knitted pullovers for a school photograph. It hung in my parent's bedroom. I kept two of his favourite toy cars.

Richie Barry was David's best friend. He named his first son David, and so did I.

15
THE SHOP

I helped in our shop during my vacations. The shop, run by my mother, was a family focal point and her control cockpit for community activities. A door led from the kitchen into the shop where a counter stretched out towards the front doors that had a bell over the top. Beside the weighing scales, there was a stretch of about four feet of open counter that was the nerve centre where all transactions with customers were carried out. Beyond that, there was a partition at head height that shielded the cash drawer and a small "office" space.

The wall behind, and parallel to, the counter had shelves that contained everything from canned vegetables and fruit, jams, candy, baking ingredients, cigarettes, and stationery, to first aid products. Outside of the counter, against the other wall, were salted cod fish hanging from the ceiling, shoes in boxes, socks, and two refrigerators, one of which held ice cream and the other bacon, sausages, and soft drinks. There was a display case with several boxes of cookies. The wall then opened up to a recessed area where, on a table and surrounding shelves, there was a dizzying variety of items from china gifts to cups and saucers, to paint, to Wellington boots and rainwear.

Freda was the first customer every day and would usually be waiting for the shop to open at 9:00 a.m. so she could buy a packet of Woodbine cigarettes. She was thin as a rake on account of paying more attention to the cigarettes than to food. Despite her nasty smoker's cough and a slight stoop, she was healthy and tough with a ruddy face and short straight hair. She lived around the corner and would often visit several times a day. No list for her.

"Back home again, Billy? Are you still going to school?" said Freda one morning. This question would be intended to "take the piss," as nobody here put a value on education.

"Gimme my packet of Bines," she said. "I'll have a bag of sugar too and a packet of sausages. Did you hear about the trouble in Goleen last night?" she asked.

"No," said I, though I had heard something, but wanted to hear her version.

"There were two of them thrown out of the dance in the Hall," she said.

"What did they do?" I asked, even though I knew she was going to tell me anyway.

"They were drunk and annoying some girls," she said, wagged her head, and headed off.

Betty, another regular customer, was a cousin of my mothers who had also married into Toormore. She was small, alert, an encyclopedia of family and local history, and a great talker. She told me more about my family history than I learned from either of my parents. Two of her sons, Andy and Richie, were playmates of mine.

Tom was an eccentric farmer who lived on his own. His clothes looked as if they did not have much acquaintance with water; this was validated by the smell that accompanied him. He would drive into the shop yard with the booming noise of a broken muffler and stop his car in front of the shop by standing on the brakes, like a rodeo rider trying to control a runaway horse. The car seemed to be held together with twine—around lights, bumpers, the silencer, and anything that could move. He needed reading glasses but never had them, so when he came into the shop, he would hold up a newspaper close to his eyes to figure out what was going on. He liked bread more than a day old; he would squeeze the loaves with his dark hands and often take three or four.

Some local customers expected the shop to be a bank of sorts. My mother kept notebooks for many customers where she entered up their groceries, and they paid monthly. There were always a few who never paid on time and when they did later, they already had a new amount in the book and so they were in a permanent loan situation.

"Why don't you hunt them up, Mom?" I asked.

"I have done but the main offenders take no notice," she said. "What can I do?"

Conversation in this small shop was expected rather than optional. While the barman has always been known to be a confidant and counselor, the small shopkeeper also filled a similar role at that time. Many customers lived in isolation and relied on their weekly visits to get an update on local and world news and divulge their issues and expect empathy and a kind word.

16

ELECTRIC TELEPHONE

In the mid-sixties, my mother was asked to take on the services of the post office in the area. She handled items such as weekly old-age pensions, social assistance, and selling stamps. A telephone was installed for use by the public.

My introduction to the phone started when I was four when my uncle Dick, at Carrigmanus, had a three-party shared line and a wind-up phone. One ring, the incoming call was for him, and two and three rings for the other two neighbours, respectively. All of this went through the postmistress, Anne, at the manual exchange in the local village of Goleen. She was known to be nosey and liked to know everyone's business. My uncle and the others on the party line assumed she regularly listened to their calls. I once heard him on the phone punctuating his comments every so often by asking, "What do you think of that Anne?" to let her know that he assumed she was a silent participant.

My uncle also showed me how to put the phone down very gently if somebody else was on the line when he picked it up. That way, the other party would not hear a click indicating that there was an eavesdropper.

Years later, wooden poles and lines were installed for the first time in Toormore. My father refused to take the phone. "What do we need that for, Nan?" he said to my mother. "If they want to talk to us, they know where we are."

My mother signed up behind his back, illustrating how democracy worked in our home. My father accepted the decision grudgingly but saw no need to speak to the plastic instrument just because it wished to speak to him. He refused to rush to answer this invader and he retorted to my mother once, "No friend of mine would be ringing me."

The arrival of the post office and public telephone heralded a new era in the shop. The problem was that most of the customers were wary of using it and expected my mother to operate it for them. She would regularly make calls to the doctor, the vet, the priest, and others, as directed by the customers. One day, Willie came into the shop and asked her to call the vet. Willie had a small farm about a mile away by a lovely beach. He was a real gentleman and shy. When she went to hand him the phone, he shook his head saying, "You are good at that sort of thing, Nan."

"What's the problem, Willie?" she asked.

"Me calf is sick," he answered.

"Willie's calf is sick," she said into the phone, having got the vet on the line.

There was a small pause, then she covered the mouthpiece with her hand and said,

"The vet wants to know what exactly is the problem?"

"He hasn't eaten anything for the last three days," Willie said, twisting furiously the hat in his hand and getting red in the face. The strained three-way conversation proceeded like this until the vet gave him a diagnosis and treatment. At the end, Willie referred in awe to the "electric telephone," his way of expressing reverence for the magical powers of the instrument, using the adjective as a validator of the newfangled invention.

17

HIPPIES

In the sixties, West Cork became one of the first centres in Ireland for hippie communes. The numbers increased during the late sixties and seventies when Timothy Leary's "Turn on, tune in, drop out" became the slogan of many young people. Typically, from middle-class families in England, they were trying to get far away from their urban experiences and values. Our region ultimately became the main centre. Some, of course, didn't last more than the first winter but the majority stuck it out.

A dentist from Bristol visited and asked my mother one day would she keep her eye on his daughter and if she was going hungry, give her food and he would pay. My mother willingly accepted the hippie-sitting task as part of her customer outreach. She sent me up the mountain one day to deliver a propane tank to the young woman, her partner, and their baby. Their house stood in a lonely area with no other signs of life in the vicinity. There was no glass in the upstairs windows, just sheets of see-through plastic. The baby was sitting on the floor with no diaper happily eating cold mackerel out of a dog's bowl. The couple was in a state of bliss. No concern for the dentist's daughter at that time. A group had a house near Toormore and bought the organ from a local church that was closing down. Their music could frequently be heard by passers-by on the main road to Schull. Another small group stayed in an Indian tepee erected near the Altar Church.

The small town of Ballydehob, and its hinterland, ten miles away, was the epicentre of activity, and Gabe's pub the meeting place. I was there one Christmas Eve and counted two locals among thirty-six "foreigners." One summer, a guy who had been thrown out by his wife from their farmhouse in the hills behind the town was sleeping in the old cowhouse, across the farmyard from the house, and he would invite everyone in the pub to go there. The same guy was reputed to be in charge of a drug supply chain link between Morocco and Spain and he disappeared at times to manage his assets.

There was little interaction at first between the hippies and the locals who tended to look askance at what they considered their aberrant behaviour. However, over time, I think they were a positive addition to the community and helped the locals open up to a broader worldview. Many craft industries were started by them. Two lesbian batik artists, for example, had a store in Ballydehob, and my mother said, "Isn't it good for a change to see two nice girls living together?"

18

DEATH

Death was accepted as an integral part of life in rural Ireland. My mother was one of the few in our area who laid out bodies for the two-day wake, a role she took on without fuss or emotion. "Someone has to do it, Billy," she said to me once when I asked her why.

In our own house, my mother had laid out many family members and organized many wakes. My mother's much older unmarried sister, May, who was mid-wife at my birth, expressed interest in the possibility of spending her last days in Toormore, but another sister, Liz, warned my mother of the potential trouble that would ensue. My mother was annoyed at Liz' comments.

"I have put down five from this house already," she retorted, "and another one isn't going to make a difference."

She was referring to both my grandparents on my father's side, her mother, and two of the Williamson cousins who moved in from their home nearby when they were no longer able to take care of themselves.

I was in my early twenties and happened to be on vacation from Dublin the morning Mrs. Dempsey died. She lived across the road from our home and her son, Tommy, arrived at our door, saying, "Nan, come quick, Mammy took a bad turn."

With Tommy leading, I followed my mother running up the laneway, in the door, to the kitchen, and up the stairs. She took one look in the doorway of Mrs. Dempsey's bedroom, turned around, and said, "Tommy, your mother is dead." Sugar-coating was not her strong point. He disappeared down the stairs in paroxysms of tears. In the meantime, she moved into action. "Billy," she said, "Get me the enamel basin and the Bible."

The tools of her trade included this enamel basin for hot water to wash the fresh corpse, scissors to cut nails, pennies to keep the eyes shut, and a Bible for under the chin until rigor mortis set in. Some families preferred to dress the corpse in pyjamas, but the majority used the deceased's Sunday best suit or dress. In this case, it was a preliminary layout procedure before the ambulance arrived to take her away to the morgue.

When I arrived back with the basin and some of the other paraphernalia, my mother took the Protestant Bible and put it under Mrs. Dempsey's chin but then asked me to go find a Catholic Bible to replace it. She was sensitive to not being branded as a proselytizer for a religion she knew Catholics viewed with distaste. I headed out to the barnyard and lit a cigarette. There was no hurry because I knew no self-respecting Catholic in Toormore would have a Bible, never mind a Catholic Bible. Protestants put great emphasis on the Bible, while Catholics did not but relied more on tradition for guidance.

I was overwhelmed with memories of Mrs. Dempsey. She was the only person in our rural area of West Cork given the honour of being called "Mrs." since she had come from a foreign and exotic land. She regaled us all as children with stories of town cricket played in Carlow, all of 120 miles to the north. I can still see the cricket game as she described it, with the local butcher puffing up over the hill to bowl to the squire of the manor. And there is Mrs. Dempsey as a young woman serving tea and cucumber sandwiches to the men in whites as they paused in their all-day game. I loved this woman and her stories.

She also told me of her marriage. Jack, then her husband to be, was a policeman with the Royal Irish Constabulary (RIC) in 1918 and was warned by the IRA that he would be killed if he didn't leave the country. The RIC was perceived to represent the British, with which the IRA was waging a guerilla war leading up to independence in 1921. The couple got married quietly during this period and he went off to the US. He had to stay there for over two years until peace had been brokered at home. During this time, Mrs. Dempsey, who was nineteen, hung her wedding ring around her neck hidden inside her clothes until he returned. She weathered challenging times as a newlywed and undercover wife of a policeman, worrying that the IRA would find out her status; she also missed her husband far away.

My last memory of Jack was about ten years before Mrs. Dempsey's death. He was in Bantry Hospital, sixteen miles away. Mrs. Dempsey told me he had the yellow "jaunders." I was home on vacation from Dublin just after he was admitted and I offered to take her and Jack's brother, Jim, to visit. Jim was a tough nut and could only see out of one eye. He said he had business to do with Jack. In the hospital, I sensed Jack was dying and that he knew it. I think he could have wished to discuss it with Mrs. Dempsey, but daren't, because it was apparent that she was in denial. After an hour of small talk, us on either side of the bed, Jim appeared in the door smelling of porter. Before he even got to the bed, he squeezed his bad eye, glared out of the other, and blurted, "Jack, where do you want to be buried?"

Jack looked forlornly at Mrs. Dempsey who had started to cry, and then back to Jim. After a silence, they agreed on the burial plan and went on to conduct some further business, as the imminent death was now out in the open. Mrs. Dempsey eventually joined in and reclaimed her position of wife in control.

I came out of my nostalgia and went back and told my mother I couldn't find a Catholic Bible anywhere. She thought for a moment and then she took the Protestant bible from under the chin where the binding showed out. She turned it around and replaced it under the chin with the leaves facing out, so now nobody would know whether it was Catholic or Protestant. I marveled at my mother's pragmatism and ingenuity and wondered whether Mrs. Dempsey, Catholic chin on Protestant Bible, would go to heaven?

19

THREE AMIGOS

Every week, Andrew, Mac, and Timmy had a ritual get-together in Goleen, the nearest village, where they collected their weekly pensions.

Andrew, known as Andrew the Waver, as his father had been a weaver, (pronounced waver), had been the postman as long as I knew him. He had a lovely, open, easygoing manner. He cut my father's hair outside our backdoor and was his barber for many years. My father claimed if you asked him a question to which he was not sure of the answer, he would respond: "I could not say for that, in case I may tell a lie." While he had a house up the side of the hill, in his later years he had taken to staying in a caravan down near the water.

Mac was a brother of Pats, both equally small and stout. Pats lived in a small house at one end of Toormore, while Mac also lived in his own small house at the other end of the townland. Nobody was ever invited or entered either house. The rare few who got a glimpse inside reported comparisons to the black hole of Calcutta. Most times Mac and Pats did not talk to each other. Washing was not a priority and sometimes it would have been easy to presume that Mac had emerged from a coalmine. He was all-knowing and when the first man landed on the moon, he did not believe it was real. He told my father: "Tom, you know how difficult it would be for us to dock our two boats together out in the bay, so how could they do it at such speed?"

Timmy was very smart. He could fix any mechanical machine or implement and was generous to a fault. For many years he drove a fish lorry from Schull to Dublin, via Castletownbere and back, on a weekly basis. He stayed with his mother, and eventually, like the other two, he lived alone with drink providing temporary comfort.

I picked up on this story from Timmy and, while it represented one day, other Fridays followed the same template. The three amigos met in Goleen mid-morning this Friday when they got their pensions. They then settled into McCarthy's bar for their first pints. The bar was mixed in with a haberdashery store, where your elbow rested on the socks while you were imbibing. The proprietor, Sean, was a philosopher king and made pronouncements from behind the counter. "In a public toilet, incoming traffic has right of way," was one of his absolute truths. Then they progressed to O'Meara's, which also doubled as a general store. Then, onwards to Coughlan's bar. Here, Finbarr ruled with a heavy hand; if he didn't like the look of a customer, he was apt to tell him where to go, with colourful expletives.

When the boys had sampled and approved of what Goleen had to offer, they took the 2:00 p.m. bus to Schull. They then got into serious drinking, first at Arundel's on the south side of the street. Then they made their way down to Newman's; it had doors leading out onto two separate streets at right angles that had disoriented many a man after a heavy feed of porter.

Finally, they finished up at Griffin's on the north side. This was Timmy's home pub, as he had known the family for years because of a fish business connection, and it had also the convenience of being the bus stop and so no worries about missing the last bus west at 9:00 p.m. Then they got back to Andrew's caravan to finish off the evening. One evening Pats, who was with them that day, got off the bus near his own home and fell into a ditch at the side of the road. A neighbor passing by pulled him out and helped him up the slope to his door.

Afterwards, Pats exclaimed: "Is there no privacy or respect anymore; can a man not get to his own home unhindered?"

20
LONDON

I finished secondary school in the summer of 1967 and decided to embark on my first trip out of Ireland before going on to university in the fall. My friend, Duncan, a few years older, had already gone to work in London the previous year; he was going again this year, and so I was happy to tag along with him with the hope of making some money for the year ahead.

We took the boat from Cork to Fishguard, in Wales. Air travel was exorbitantly expensive in those days, and besides, I was keen to sample the method of transport taken by thousands of emigrants over the century past. It was an overnight trip mainly populated by Irishmen returning to the UK after their meager but long-anticipated holiday at home. As the night moved on there was a variety of songs but predominately mournful nationalist ballads. The bonhomie was forced as most were upset about leaving family and many possibly realizing that the UK would become their permanent home. Thoughts of relocating to Ireland were only a pipe dream. My abiding memory—apart from the emotional punch of the songs— was of the deck awash with booze, punctuated in places with sick. I found the whole situation sad and also felt lucky that I was on an educational trajectory that should insulate me from this traditional forced emigration.

We took the train from Fishguard. On arrival in London, we went straight to the West Kensington area, and to Stanley Boyden at 6 Hazlett Road. Duncan had stayed with him the previous year, and Stanley met us at the door and welcomed him back. He ran a boarding house in a three-story Victorian red-brick house in a quiet street of similar houses, elegant but past their heyday. He was thin and gaunt and not easy to engage with, because, while he also lived in the house, he was somewhat reclusive; I could go days without seeing him. We were allocated a room in the basement with two single beds. It was small and squalid with one tiny window to the outside ground level, set high in the wall. The only redeeming feature was the low price.

Lyons Bakery was a short walk away and I managed to get employment there. I was allocated to the Test Market Department where a few products were run to test consumer reaction, if positive they would allocate the product to another department and to a permanent production line. I was put at the end of a long oven. The products were mainly apple pies and my job was to remove them in trays and place them in a large rack on wheels. Another worker pulled it away when it was full.

This was my first experience of multiculturalism. There was only one other white student among about thirty staff. I had good relations with all but I never got to socializing with them. After work, they headed for home, and so did I. The work was quite boring and onerous in that I had to remove the pies immediately as they emerged from the oven because, otherwise, they would pile up on the floor. However, the biggest challenge was being at the end of a hot oven during an unusually strong July heat wave outside. More than once I felt sorry for these guys confined to their menial jobs while again counting my blessings to be on the university track.

There were no hygiene routines at work, partly I suppose because everything was temporary due to the fact of being a test market department. The oven ran close to, and parallel with, the wall, and one guy, too lazy to go to the toilet, used to piss behind it on a regular basis.

To earn some extra money, I sometimes worked an evening shift at Walls Ice cream beside Lyons. The job consisted of packing four large sealed cylindrical cans of ice cream in custom-sized cardboard boxes. Before starting work, we had to wash our hands thoroughly, despite the fact that the product was sealed; the comparison to Lyons, where we were dealing with exposed products, was interesting.

On Saturday mornings, I would usually head downtown to see the sights and experience the buzz of one of the greatest cities in the world. West Kensington was the closest subway station and I was in awe of the efficiency of this mode of transport. I went to Portobello Road one Saturday morning to take in the famous street market. Apart from clothing stalls, for which it was renowned, there was a myriad of other products, and the street was thick with people dressed in wild colours and styles. We were in the middle of the flower-power hippie era and flamboyance was the norm. I bought a trick pack of cards and a transistor radio, both of which gave me long service, and which I still have today.

Downtown had so many great sights for an awestruck Irish youth—the magnificent Houses of Parliament stretching like a gingerbread ornament along the Thames, with the towering Big Ben overhead; the beauty and serenity of St. Paul's Cathedral and Westminster Abbey. They all need to be seen to be believed. Trafalgar Square was also a favourite and I particularly enjoyed Speakers' Corner at Hyde Park, where at the weekend there was a long-standing custom of free speech from a soapbox. Large crowds would gather and cheer on or heckle the speaker. Most speakers were anti-establishment, forceful, and entertaining. Jacobus Van Dynn was one of the more notable characters. He appeared with a naked upper body, no hair, and totally covered with tattoos—including all over his head and face. I did not have the self-confidence or courage at that time to get up and perform to the public. However, I derived great enjoyment from hearing dissenting voices.

Somewhere towards the end of July, I noticed I was suffering from homesickness and depression although I would not have had enough self-awareness then to use such descriptions. While on one level, I loved being in London, I was working long, strenuous and mindless hours and did not have anyone to talk to in the evening in our uninviting room, as Duncan was working late shifts. I lost energy and enthusiasm to do anything and obsessed about missing a precious summer at home in Toormore. Eventually, I decided I had to go, feeling guilty about abandoning Duncan, but it was something I had to do to regain my peace of mind.

I decided on the way home to stop for a few days in Gloucestershire to visit some cousins and friends. As soon as I got on the bus westward, I began to feel better and was in top form again during my visit. I left them in great spirits as I made the final bus trip to the boat in Fishguard. When I arrived home to Toormore my parents were glad to see me. I got into helping my mother in the shop and enjoyed the remainder of the summer like I had all those previous.

21
CROOKHAVEN

I had my first experience of drinking at Sonny's Pub in Crookhaven.

Crookhaven was ten miles from my home in Toormore and my best friend, Tom, and I were regulars there in our late teens and early twenties. In fact, at times we were daily communicants. One summer, throughout July and August, I estimate we never got to bed before 2:00 a.m., and often later.

The village is in a spectacular setting on a peninsula at the side of a large bay. As I drove around the bay, I brought to mind that in the late eighteen hundreds I'd heard there were so many ships at anchor that you could walk across the bay on the decks.

Sonny had a way of playfully insulting customers, as he stood behind the bar with his cap at a slant, elbows on the counter, and a wicked smile. A favourite trick of his, if he was asked a question he thought stupid, was to just stare at the customer. He was at an age where he didn't care much about business anymore, while his son, Billy, took over. We drank pints of beer and got to know the locals and some of the holidaymakers.

Jinks was one of the high-profile locals; he had a ruddy complexion and only a few front teeth that protruded at different angles. He was a known rogue who lived off his wits; caging pints from tourists was one of his specialties. In the early sixties, MGM made a movie in the village and its surroundings, named *I Thank a Fool.* Peter Finch was the male lead and he invited Jinks to stay with him for the duration in his rented cottage. Suitable accommodation was limited; while the rest of the actors stayed in a hotel many miles away, Finch had decided to sample the local experience. Every morning, Jinks went down to Sonny's to replenish the drink supply, all charged up to MGM. He was in his element. I was talking one day to the old lady who rented the house to them and she said the back yard was so full of bottles at the end of their stay she had to get a truck to haul them away.

"Daddy" Nottage was in his nineties and ran one of the other two pubs. He had come from Cornwall as a young man to work on the local Marconi tower, married a local girl, and never left. Very few people drank in his pub at this stage and he often left his place open and went down to Sonny's for a drink himself. Tom and I frequently went into his place for a first drink. One evening, Daddy was missing so Tom plugged in the kettle, made us both hot whiskeys, and we left the cash on the counter.

Pat Murphy was a non-native retiree. He had been a journalist with the *Daily Mail* and regaled us with many stories of his world adventures. He claimed to have been in Russia in 1917 for the revolution, and indeed he was old enough to have been. He related stories about the Bolsheviks in St. Petersburg in graphic detail. He also talked of walking with pilgrims from London to Rome in the Marion year of 1950 when Catholics converged to celebrate the Pope's new dogma that the Virgin Mary was assumed directly into heaven. Pat was a fluent bullshitter, but an articulate and very funny one.

Flor was my favourite. He always shuffled in like he hoped not to be noticed, with his deathly pale face under his cap. He was shy and self-effacing and took a while to get to know. He was very smart with broad interests and his knowledge of unusual ballads was astounding. He had a huge repertoire of mainly unaccompanied songs like the twenty-minute multi-verse *Dingle Puck Goat* and *Miss Gilhooley's Party.* I would name a song and he would start immediately, with his thin, reedy voice accompanied by a tapping foot.

And then there were the younger tourists like us. Tom was tall, blond, and good looking and generally got the first pick of the female crop. I had learned to be happy with second choice but the odd time I would get in front of Tom using a little cunning. One evening he was holding forth to a prospect and I noticed she strongly disagreed with his position on the war in Vietnam. When he went to the toilet, I brought the subject back up and said, "You made a good point there on Vietnam." She looked pleased. The thrill of competing was nearly wiped out by the fear of him finding out. She had long hair, a cute face, and legs that went up to her neck. Unfortunately, she was another who got away, but the process was fun.

As the evening moved on, we tended to graduate to contemporary songs with piano and guitar accompaniment, depending on who was available. When Sonny finally called closing time, instead of singing the National Anthem, our favourite lung-buster was *Delilah,* a full-throttle version popularized by the Welsh heartthrob, Tom Jones. Of course, closing time was a moveable feast depending on Sonny's mood. I think official closing at that time was about 11:00 but Sony was likely to extend this until 1:00 or 2:00 a.m. if the "craic" was good. When he decided to close, he was wont to say, "I have yer money, ye have yer piss, now fuck off and leave me alone."

Not only did I learn to drink at Sonny's, but also, I unwittingly learned how to delay the first visit to the toilet. I discovered this years later when I was dating a young woman in Dublin and one evening, sitting in a pub, she leaned over and conspiratorially asked, "Do you mind if I ask you a personal question?" I was horrified with the fear that she would comment on body odour, nose picking, or a myriad of other bad personal habits. I felt I had no choice, and said, "go ahead."

"Why do you never have to go for the first piss?" she said. "I notice that I may have to go three or four times before you do." It took a while to get over the shock and to realize she was quite admiring of this skill.

It was later that I figured out the probable cause. In Sonny's, especially in winter, storytelling was at its peak and there were two reasons I resisted going—one was the possibility of missing the end of a good story, and more importantly, it required going out the front door, facing the elements, and around the side, to relieve myself against the wall. The particular hue of green of the wall depended on how many men had ministered to it in recent times. I would be bent down in discomfort to avoid either or both of these catastrophes and never realized that someday the experience would bring me a certain kind of athletic prowess.

22

REGATTA

A centerpiece of the summer for Crookhaven was the regatta in August, quite a tourist attraction, and a big social occasion for the locals. The organizers had to use ingenuity to tailor activities suitable for the limited resources available. On the day, as I arrived in the early afternoon, I spotted Jinks furiously sawing a board to make a fourth seat for the Crookhaven boat for the rowing race. The other team had come all the way from Long Island with a four-seater boat. "We can't let them go home without a race," said Jinks, explaining his extra seat. Unsurprisingly, the Long Island men won easily, but honour had been saved.

There was an outboard motor race I remember best, with a dozen boats lining up at the starting line. There was a mixture of types of boat but what caught my attention was a huge motorboat that dwarfed the rest, its captain kitted out with naval officer cap and blazer to face the challenge ahead. At the starter's gun, they all headed off to the best of their abilities.

The captain immediately jumped way ahead. There was one small lonely punt with a two-and-a-half horsepower motor sputtering away on the stern and everyone left him behind. As the captain rounded the buoy for the return run, the organizer announced on his megaphone: “First around the buoy, all turn around.” Because the small punt had made so little progress, he made it home first and the captain finished up last. It was a classic case of “the last shall be first.” Crookhaven makes its own rules, but I don’t think the captain was amused.

23

ALTAR STONE

The South and West of Ireland have a great selection of prehistoric relics that are mainly unappreciated by the locals. There are two dolmens in my townland of Toormore. These consist of three large raised stones at each side and an even larger stone on top, at a slight slope from the horizontal, like a leaning prehistoric crab. They are megalithic tombs dating from 4000 to 3000 BC.

It remains unclear when, why, and by whom the earliest dolmens were made. The oldest known are found in Western Europe, dating from circa 7,000 years ago. Archaeologists still do not know who erected these dolmens, which makes it difficult to know why they did. They are generally regarded as tombs or burial chambers, despite the absence of clear evidence for this.

None of this we knew as children as we used the Altar Stone as just another prop for our play. Climbing up the side stones to get to the top flat stone was a challenge, and having mastered this, we danced around for hours while looking out to the nearby sea. When it rained, we were able to shelter inside the vertical stones at the sides and under the large top stone. While initially we had no knowledge of the history, we had a sense of the majesty and dignity of the place. It was on the edge of Toormore Bay with a view out to the Atlantic Ocean. In summer the surroundings bloomed with flaming orange montbretia and fuchsia in its purple and scarlet glory. Nobody interrupted us; nobody visited the Stone.

Years later, I visited again. The road from Schull, the nearest town, went through typical West Cork terrain, a combination of bare rocks and boggy patches of fields. At the top of Grans Hill, I saw my first glimpse of the sea heralding that home was not far away. Finally, I rounded the "sea turn" and there was Toormore Bay in front, and on the left, built on rocks that moved gradually down to the water, was the Altar Stone. I stopped because I saw a new car park had been opened up right beside the stone. I did a quick look around; everything appeared in order, and as I left, I felt happy that it was now easier for more people to access and marvel at the stone.

During my stay, I made enquiries about the origin of the car park and found a more interesting story. A professor of archeology at the University of Cork had started a program of digs, primarily for American students. While there is a relative profusion of dolmens in Ireland, I immediately understood the attraction for these students to be able to work on some pre-historic artifacts, and how profitable it could be for the university. A local farmer was asked to use his tractor and lifting gear to lift off the flat stone that was several tons weight, presumably to make digging easier underneath, although there was plenty of room to dig underneath without molesting the stone. When they were finished, they filled back the earth and replaced the stone.

Nobody would notice that there was any change. But to me, that wasn't the point; I knew that the stone had been moved. While most things have changed in modern Ireland, I had foolishly assumed that "our" stone was a constant, and the thought that this magnificent relic had survived 3,000, or probably more, years to be molested by some modern-day Philistines was appalling for me. I heard later that nothing of significance was found, and this was also the case for many previous digs. So why did they have to assault our stone, and certainly without any effort to get local opinion?

I could not get it out of my head, and every time I passed afterward, even though it looked the same, I could not stop my thoughts of anger. To me, the Altar Stone represents one of the few constants of my home area and is diminished by an act of vandalism, all for filthy lucre. They molested me, my youth, and my friends. Nothing is sacred, and nothing is untouchable in the land of saints and scholars.

24

PATH TO UNIVERSITY

Because I was young, I had already been held back a year to do my Intermediate State Exam again at fifteen. Still young at seventeen, when I did the final year Leaving Certificate Exam, the headmaster suggested I come back another year to prepare for going to university. Everyone presumed, including me, I would be going to university, but without any clear idea of how I would fund it. My parents certainly couldn't afford it.

Career guidance involved three or four of us being marked out for university, five or six expected to go back to the family farm, and the remainder aimed towards commerce in Cork. The headmaster had contacts in insurance and the banks, predominately, where the Protestant presence was still strong. In the case of Rich, one Sunday, the headmaster drove us halfway to our home to meet our parents on the bridge in Bandon. I sat with my uncle in his car while my parents and Rich met with the headmaster in his car. He outlined what he thought was a suitable opportunity at a large grain importer with a Protestant ethos. Rich went for an interview, got the job, and subsequently had a very successful career with them. Such was career guidance in those days. Through all our time together, Rich never showed any envy of my slightly better academic performance and that I, but not he, was on the university track. We both took it as a reality that didn't merit dispute and I appreciated that he never made this a bone of contention.

Two of my school colleagues were aiming for university like me, but their finances were secure. We were all planning to study for the UK "A" Levels, which were a step above the Leaving and would thus prepare us better for university.

Having started on this plan, at the beginning of my final year, the headmaster took me aside one day:

"I have looked again at your Leaving results and realized that they're good enough to win a county council scholarship—if you had taken and got a reasonable mark in an Honours Irish paper."

Irish had to feature among four other subjects in the portfolio for assessment. This was one of a number of political gestures at the time to encourage the resurrection of the language. I had a more than average grasp of Irish and liked the language. However, I was mindful I would be up against some who were fluent and did all their subjects through Irish, and also of the fact there were only twenty scholarships awarded for the whole county. It was an all-or-nothing bet because if I didn't win one, I would have nothing to show for the year. At the same time, pursuing "A" Levels would have some academic benefit but no solution to the

finance. I decided to take my chances and go for the Leaving again, including the Irish.

My Irish teacher volunteered to give me extra tutoring. We met regularly in a small office under the stairs in a new residential building. It was tough going and I owed him a lot for sticking with me. I had estimated I needed a minimum of seventy on the paper if I could keep my other marks in the high eighties and low nineties, like in the previous year.

Harder than the Irish grinds was worrying about maintaining the marks in the other subjects. It was tempting to assume this would be easy, so I tried hard to treat each subject like I was approaching it new. One initiative I took was to get up early in the morning before the official time to get an extra hour of study to start the day. I have never been more motivated and worked harder in my life than in the months of early 1967 leading up to the Leaving Cert exams in June. The only future I focused on was getting that scholarship to go to university.

This was made easier, of course, because there was little temptation of outside socializing. When the time for the exams arrived, I was as well prepared as I could be. I was always a reasonably good exam candidate in that, despite some inevitable tension leading up to the start, once it began, I was calm and never panicked. My main weakness was that I tended to be too wordy and didn't always get finished in time. I did not commit any major goofs and by the end of the exams, I felt I had given my best.

During the final term, I had applied for a new sponsorship scheme in engineering at Trinity College, Dublin, where five companies had signed up to take a candidate each; they would cover the fees, while the student worked with the company during vacations. I interviewed and was accepted by a company in the concrete business. This would require me to do civil engineering rather than my choice of electronics, but in my mind, it was a reasonable compromise as a backup if I didn't win the scholarship.

I stayed close to home that summer and spent a good deal of time worrying about my future. The Leaving Cert results were always issued in the middle of August, so it was a long wait for me. The letter finally arrived. I sat for a long time looking at it and turning it over in my hand again and again. I eventually plucked up the courage to open it and read that I was one of the twenty. My reaction was more relief than elation; many people had put their faith in me and I was glad to have met their expectations. Also, the "all-or-nothing" bet I had made to re-do the exams had been a strain. I had exceeded my target mark in Irish, and the marks in the other subjects had exceeded the previous year. I had a great sense of achievement.

I now had one final decision to make—what to do about the agreement with the potential sponsor company. The scholarship deal was better in the sense that it gave me freedom of specialization and freedom to do what I wanted during vacation time. However, I was afraid to renege on my agreement. In the end, I resolved to tell them the truth about the situation. I stood in a payphone box in Schull, the nearest town, with my mother outside for support. I dropped the coins reluctantly one by one. When I got the executive on the line, he was not sympathetic to my story. He showed no interest in my circumstances. His main gripe was that it was now too late for him to get a replacement, although subsequently, he did get someone. I also got a lecture about not starting out in life by breaking agreements.

I was very naïve and felt embarrassed and at fault.

DUBLIN

25

THE RANCH

My first accommodation in Dublin, when I went to university in the fall of 1967, was at the Harding Boys Home. The Ranch, as the inmates knew it, had upwards of 50 young male residents. Its official purpose was to be a home for young Protestant working boys from the country coming to Dublin for the first time. The food and board were basic, but so was the rent. The typical young man finished school, left the cocoon of his family, and came to the city to make his name in retail, insurance, or banking. The Ranch also accepted some university students like me, no more than a dozen at any one time. While I had been away from home at boarding school for years, this was also a new beginning for me. I was both excited and nervous of what lay ahead.

An elegant 5-storey Victorian red brick building, the Ranch stood at the top of Dame Street, beside Christchurch Cathedral, a 20 minute-walk from the front gates of Trinity College. The imposing entrance had large double wooden doors that opened into a big square hallway, from which a wide staircase wound upwards to the top of the building. A pulsing life beat behind these high walls and doors, only visible to the insiders.

The manager, Dudley Dolan, had big round glasses and a large mustache that was shaped like buffalo horns. He looked and sounded like an army officer who supported the idea of forcing the Africans to become good citizens of the British Empire. On the other hand, he could have been a headmaster of a secondary school in need of discipline. Nobody knew his background. He had many regulations, never written, and was rarely approached by an inmate, as discussion wasn't part of his army-like repertoire. Dudley's wife, Dolly, was an able back up and a strict authoritarian figure in her own right. She was small and round with a face like an East German Stazi on patrol. One of her main duties was to ensure Dudley got a full house for his Sunday school classes.

The atmosphere fell somewhere between a boarding school and a youth detention centre, a perfect launching pad for me as an innocent abroad in a big city. The average inmate had escaped his mother's clutches but she could be consoled by the fact that there was, at least, some imposed discipline, and most of all a guaranteed full stomach. I learnt to live with, or circumvent, the rules, as a small nuisance in exchange for the beguiling whiff of freedom. I was coming from a restricted boarding school background with very little knowledge of a larger world, and so this semi-chaperoned situation was ideal for me.

We all lined up at a hatch on one side of the dining room to get our food from a little old lady, who lived on the premises and was reputed to be heavy on the bottle. One day, a fellow student dropped his plate and food all over the floor. The first reaction was cheers and a burst of applause from the gathered inmates, more in the style of a reform institution than a boarding school.

The rules included having a door key for no more than 3 nights per week. Some thwarted the key problem by climbing up a downpipe at the back of the building. In the larger dormitories sleep was often interrupted by a few of the regular carousers on their way home from the pub. My bed was near the door at one end of the largest dormitory, while, mercifully, these guys slept at the other end of the room. The amount of noise made as they passed to their beds depended on their degree of intoxication. Half way along the dormitory there was an unfortunate victim who must have displeased them at some stage. They would regularly shout with increasing volume, "Are you asleep, Jeffrey? Are you asleep, Jeffrey? Fuck ya, answer me,", and if necessary, they would grab his ankle and shake until they got a response.

At the end of this long dormitory that stretched to one end of the building, there was a window through which we could access the flat roof of the residence next door. In the summer I, and a few friends, took to using this roof as our private sunbathing perch. After a while we decided to pioneer the "one sock" method of sunbathing, the sock being a concession to the sensitivity of the male member. Unfortunately, we had not realized that we could be seen from a taller office building across the street, and someone decided that his or her moral code was being violated, and made a complaint to Dolan. We had been forbidden to ever trespass on the roof next door, never mind indulge in the "one sock" activity, and so we decided our only option was to vociferously deny any knowledge of both charges. I hung on with all my courage when Dolan confronted us, as I was aware that one of the possible consequences of guilt was expulsion. By now I had hardened my mindset into breaking the rules and denial without proof. We succeeded in escaping all Dolan's threats, as of course there was no evidence and, as we guessed, no willing witnesses to make allegations about the cut of our members.

One evening on our way home from Trinity a few student friends and I noticed a commotion outside the Olympia theatre, on Dame Street. Paul Golden, the then-famous hypnotist, was appearing for a week. The next evening my friend Mervyn and I went along to the show. At the appropriate time, Mervyn and I volunteered to go on stage with about 20 others. While I had an open mind about the possibility of hypnotism, it became apparent slowly that Golden put on a clever show for the audience. If somebody did not obey his orders he would ask them to leave the stage "You have too strong a mind, I can't hypnotise you," he would say, thus not humiliating the would-be volunteer. His technique included telling the audience what we would do after he hypnotized us, but of course this was also letting us know what he expected after he did his voodoo. At one stage he put us all lying on the stage while he went off for a break. I began to raise my hand and slowly wave because we had two other friends in the audience and I had promised to try to give them a sign at some stage that I wasn't hypnotized. I became aware of movement off-stage and I saw Golden gesticulating in my direction. "Put your hand down. Put your hand down. Put your hand down," he hissed. When he later resumed the act, I noticed he did not approach me any more with special instructions because I suppose he didn't trust me. In the finale to the show, he would direct all the hypnotized volunteers to rush out onto the street looking for green leprechauns, and onto the open-door double deck buses. Did we need any more incentive to cause chaos, without risk of arrest? The final bonus is that we all got free passes for the next show. As a result, Mervyn and I went along for the next 4 or 5 days, and when Golden saw that we were such devout followers, he took us back into his group of favourites.

Playing cards and discussing politics, often at the same time, were two of my favourite hobbies. A small group of us would play cards at lunch, before dinner, and again in the evening. We oscillated between 25, 110, and poker. The first 2 games are somewhat similar to Whist and Euchre, but with a different way of valuing the cards. There were often tense moments and aggravation, but never any lasting bad feeling. Trinity was bubbling with revolutionary zeal mainly as a result of the war in Vietnam, the troubles in Northern Ireland, and the spread of Maoism and Marxism. Apart from debating these issues with great gusto, the shooting of Robert Kennedy hit us hard and deflated our student idealism.

Attendance in-house Sunday School each Sunday morning, led by Dudley himself, was mandatory, as well as going to church afterwards. I, and some others, frequently avoided this imposition on our freedom by "disappearing." A wall conveniently flanked my bed at one side of the dormitory. I would rough up the bedclothes, drag them down to the floor at the open side of the bed, and take up position underneath, behind the bedclothes. Oblivious to the fact that we were all-male interns, Dolly's policing involved visiting the dormitories to flush out malingerers for Dudley's scintillating sessions; she visited my room on a number of occasions but she never suspected my cover. I was not amused by this silly game, especially if I had been out the night before. However, the inconvenience was far less upsetting than listening to Dudley interpret the Bible.

My friend, John King, a red-bearded Marxist, and I would sometimes go to coffee houses in O'Connell Street instead of the mandatory church attendance on Sundays. In Cafolas café we would regularly meet representatives of the St. Vincent de Paul's, who were in search of lost souls. There were parallel rows of tables, divided by a partition. Two of their people would frequently sit at the table at the other side of the partition to us and try to strike up conversation. One was tall with slicked down hair and what appeared to be the same dirty shirt. The other was short and bald. We found that engaging was more fun than trying to shake them off. We took on different personas, assuming they would not be interested in talking to Protestants or Marxists.

"What are you boys doing here at this time on a Sunday?" asked the small proselytizer.

"We are new immigrants, and would like to know where there is a good church," I responded.

"Oh, the Catholic Cathedral is just down the road with masses every hour," suggested the tall smelly one. "Great," said John, "and could you tell us something about the state of the church in Ireland at the moment, what with all these student Maoists and Marxists we hear about?" And so, it went. We derived great entertainment debating their beliefs and mythology. One day the tall one took a religious icon from around his neck and gave it to me to keep me safe. I put it in the bin later as, unfortunately, it was smelly, like its donor.

Notwithstanding our protests at the mandatory church attendance, I was one of the ringleaders who frequently attended St. Anne's church in Dawson Street, rather than Cafola, with a goal more important than being saved. We sat high up in the balcony at the back, beside the magnificent organ that was played by the mad organist, Willie Watson. In front of us were a few rows of girls from the Protestant Young Women's Christian Association (YWCA), and the Girls Friendly Society (GFS), female, protestant institutions similar to the Ranch, also close to the centre of the city. This was a perfect opportunity for brokering dates. The amount of activity ebbed and flowed with the music, because talking over the prayers and sermon drew too much attention from the rest of the congregation. The majesty of the Messiah, for example, usually brought the dating arrangements to a peak.

I left the Ranch after 2 years to take up residence in Trinity for my final 2 years of university. Having got used to the big city at this stage I couldn't wait to get away from all the juvenile restrictions and soak up the freedom and excitement of campus life. However, I missed the camaraderie and the kick of finding ways to circumvent the rules.

Eventually, the Ranch was taken over and used as a youth hostel. Many years later, I walked in and upstairs to visit my old dormitory and nearly collided with a young German lady. The shock of meeting a female in what was a very male bastion was enough to propel a hasty retreat. The YWCA and GFS are also long since gone. The dating in the gallery of St. Annes is over.

26

TRINITY COLLEGE

The late sixties were an exciting time to be at Trinity College as student political protest was at its height, with anti-war Vietnam protests, and Marxists, Maoists, Trotskyites, Nationalists, and Republicans all vying for attention.

Trinity was built like an oasis in the centre of Dublin where the streets ultimately formed themselves around it. Nearly all the original buildings were intact; going in the front doors to the cobbles of the front square felt like entering another era. The first thing I was aware of as I went through the entrance was the history of this place founded in 1592, and the fact that luminaries such as Swift, Wilde, Beckett, Goldsmith, and Burke had passed through here. I was pulled back to the present by the cacophony from students on the front porch promoting everything from sports to drama and debate clubs.

I arrived at Trinity at the end of an era in Ireland, where there was a mix of Protestants from Northern Ireland, students based overseas in Commonwealth countries, and Protestants from the Republic of Ireland, as well as some Catholics. However, Catholics were in the minority, and the Catholic bishops demanded that any of their flock wishing to go had to get their permission first. This was rarely granted but many ignored the injunction and went anyway. This was great for me as I easily made new friends with Catholic students who, by definition, had a certain independence of mind, as they had already run the gauntlet of their bishop.

A friend of mine, Jim, found out belatedly he had been refused permission from his bishop. After some to-ing and fro-ing, including mediation by his father, the bishop realized that Jim had no intention of obeying his veto and sent a final reconciliatory letter outlining ten different things Jim needed to do, including going to mass weekly and not mixing with Protestants. Jim paid no attention.

The Protestants from Northern Ireland had large British grants and probably reasonably well-off parents. We, Protestants from the Republic, envied many of these as they drove around in fancy sports cars, and in general, they remained in a clique and did not mix much with others.

The returning colonials added colour. Fitzmaurice-White was a typical example, acting in a way that did justice to his double-barrel name. He was from Rhodesia, tall and good-looking with blond hair neatly combed. He comported himself with a superiority that I could imagine him ordering the Africans back home into shape.

The museum building, near the rugby and cricket pitches, was shared by the engineering and geology departments. The latter accounted for the huge skeleton of a prehistoric animal in the hallway inside the front door. The magnificent marble and granite hallway was open to the top and at the back wall; the stairs went left to geology and right to engineering. I climbed to the right. I had little trouble adjusting to engineering lectures from the secondary school model, partly because the lecturing style had been adopted by some of my teachers at school, and also, I had become accustomed to independent study. There were, of course, some lecturers who stuck slavishly to methods that may have worked once, but not then. Fitzgibbon lectured on structures by writing his notes on the board and expecting us to copy them down. Apart from the futility of this, he wrote fast, his writing was not easily legible, and this continued monotonously to the end of the hour.

Gregg, in physics, seemed to not have a strong grasp of his subject matter and would not give us any reference material. Somebody looked up when he graduated and surveyed the books published around that time to find his core reference book. We then peppered him with questions about anything we didn't immediately understand in the book on the assumption that he might have the same problem. Those of us who participated in this baiting knew we would have to work harder to ensure he couldn't fail us in the exam at the end of the term. We did two different types of math, pure and applied, two BA arts subjects, and by doing one further arts subject, we could obtain a BA degree in addition to our engineering degree. The choice of subjects was limited, so most engineering students, including me, took economics, on the assumption it would be easy to bullshit our way through.

While our engineering class had only two women, the economics class was full of all sorts of women wearing a variety of trendy clothes. The first thing I noticed is that these nice women were not too keen on the engineers' presence and avoided sitting near us when possible. The average engineer wore dirty jeans and a donkey jacket—a short jacket made from cheap fabric—and probably smelled. In any case, we were able to admire the young women from afar. Whenever the lecturer put a graph on the board, we engineers were in our element, whereas it left many of the others in a swoon by the introduction of such a mystifying tool.

I didn't understand some of the more esoteric material, but I took copious notes. The exam paper always had thirteen questions from which you had to choose just three to answer. I usually bought the professor's latest book a few weeks before the exam. I rarely got around to reading it, but the act of buying lifted my confidence. As an engineering student, with lectures every day, I envied those in BA studies with a few lectures a week and only three exams, all of which had a stupendous set of question options. But I, and most of my colleagues, always passed comfortably.

In general, at that time, I didn't think too much about anything, but over the four years, I became aware of a few things. First, the philosophy of teaching was similar to that in secondary school—memorize facts rather than encourage independent thinking and creativity. While I was credited as being "bright," my good results were primarily due to being blessed with a strong memory, supplemented by hard work.

I entered engineering because I was good in the sciences and math, and it was meant to be a channel to a good job. I choose the electronics stream as it was the most difficult academically and also, I had always enjoyed tinkering with crystal-set radios. It didn't take long to realize that the academic study of electronics had little to do with tinkering with radios. I had a suspicion that engineering had found its way under the university umbrella as a drive to make the profession respectable so new graduates could enter society at an appropriate level with no grease on their hands. I had a similar suspicion about other exalted but technically based professions such as medicine.

I hadn't yet developed a strong sense of identity, or where I wanted to go in life. Although I realized I would be far more suited to an arts program, with subjects like philosophy, psychology, and history, I hadn't the courage to make a change and was afraid of where this might lead. I couldn't displease my mother or father, because they didn't understand what I was doing anyway. As I dithered, the small window for becoming a Renaissance man closed.

Lest I give the impression it was all work, I played rugby for a while for the lowest team. I also participated in the main debating society and often dined at Commons, where academic gowns were mandatory, and Guinness provided a courtesy glass of their best to all diners. Also, I imbibed copious pints at O'Neill's pub near the front gate.

For an end-of-year rite of passage, we engineers usually celebrated with huge relief after exams were finished. By the time the results came out many weeks later, we had all dispersed to our various summer activities. At the end of my second year, more than twenty of us gathered in the early evening in Mulligan's Pub, some, including myself, having had no dinner. Mulligan's is a famous Dublin drinking establishment and features in Joyce's *Ulysses*, as well as other novels and written references. It is long and low with old woodwork and still has the old wooden floor covered with sawdust, rare in Dublin at that stage. One of the reasons we chose it was for the floor.

The barmen had a liberal attitude to spills, as distinct from more respectable pubs at that time.

We were all at a long table on the right-hand side inside the door. The drink began to flow—mainly pints of Smithwick's beer, and some Guinness. John served us. He wore an oilskin apron and good boots and was good-humoured, bearing in mind we were keeping him occupied full time.

While most of us had many with whom we were friendly, we rarely got a chance to socialize with some others. This was the one time annually that we all had an opportunity to mix and enjoy the bonhomie and bolster the bad social reputation we had as engineers. Medical and veterinary studies had similar ratings and we were always conscious of the competition and our wish to stay at the top of the tree for behavior not approved by the mainstream.

The evening progressed, and one of the group who was sitting on the outside of the table, lent back over his shoulder and got sick on the floor. John was over in a minute with a bucket and mop that he must have had ready for this eventuality. He didn't remonstrate with the perpetrator but just bent to his task as if this was a regular occurrence. From the way he was dressed, maybe it was. The sawdust soaked up most of the mess and made the mopping easier. Not too long after, another guy was running on his way to the toilet at the back when he didn't make it and spewed all over a long stretch of the floor. Again, John cleaned up without saying a word.

Coming on to closing time, I felt the bile rise and I headed for the front door with a view to not bothering John again. Unfortunately, I started to throw up as I went out the door and some of it caught the doorframe. When John arrived, looking at the doorframe more in sorrow than in anger he said: “Why didn’t you just do it on the floor, like the rest of them?”

27
ATLANTIC CITY

I made my first visit to the US in the summer of 1969, at the age of twenty. I was a student on a J1 working Visa and travelled with my buddy, Mervyn. In Ireland at that time, the States represented the shining City on the Hill where everything was bigger and better, and the Vietnam war was just an aberration.

We stayed our first night in New York and were not overly impressed by the tall buildings as we had seen them often in the movies. We decided to head for Atlantic City because the amusement piers we'd heard of sounded exotic and we were told it was good for summer jobs.

Atlantic city was mesmerizing for someone who had never been out of Ireland and England. Everything was so different—the huge crowds, the accents, and the smells. It was my first exposure to humidity, never mind the temperature. We marveled at the porches on the houses where we could sit out, the scent and taste of pancakes as well as bacon and eggs for breakfast, coffee at every turn, the sound of cicadas at night, and the consistent presence of the sun by day.

A wide wooden boardwalk stretched as far as the eye could see in both directions. There was a profusion of cafés and vendors on this esplanade selling everything from candy, cotton candy, corn, pizza, and hot dogs, to cheap souvenirs. At that time, there was limited trans-Atlantic communication and as a result, the style of dress for young Americans was quite different. I had never seen slogan T-shirts, cut-off jeans, micro-skirts, and sandals. It was an exotic destination for exploration with two long months to do so.

Eventually, Mervyn, I, and two other friends found a small apartment. It was so small that if you came in the front door too fast, you could be going out the back. Two single beds left practically no further space in each of the two rooms. Mervyn and I had the bedroom right beside the front door.

After a few anxious days searching, we were hired by the Steeplechase Pier. It was family-run and one of maybe a dozen piers extending from the boardwalk that ran for miles along the seafront. The Steeplechase Pier was one of the smallest but had its share of amusements. There were kiddie rides for the children, an overhead cable car, and a range of gambling opportunities for adults. Mervyn ended up in the stall where guests had to try to pitch three large balls into a basket so they did not bounce out again. It seemed simple but was not.

I was allocated to a stall across from Mervyn a little further along the pier. My booth had a large circular wooden dial with a range of colours around the circumference and a centre-mounted rotating arm. Guests put their dime on their colour of choice on a horizontal board, and I spun the arm to determine the winners. The payout varied from very small trinkets to very large stuffed animals.

Soon after I started work, I had an unusual experience. One day I noticed a mother and daughter lingering at my booth. In the space between guests, they told me that the previous year they were here and the guy running this booth was Irish also. Nina, the daughter, had fallen madly in love with him. They arrived every day until one day Mrs. Reinhardt told me surreptitiously, "On account of you being Irish, Nina has begun to transfer her interest to you."

Nina took me for a ride in her Mustang convertible, which made me think all my car-Christmases had come together. We'd had a few more dates when, at lunch one day with Nina and her mother at a Woolworth's food counter, the mother came out with the extraordinary proposal. "I would like you to marry my daughter," said Mrs. Reinhardt. "I suggest you transfer your studies to Philadelphia and I will cover all costs." I thought she was joking at first, but she was dead serious with Nina apparently in agreement. We hardly knew each other. They were from Philadelphia and had driven here, as they did every year. Nina was an only child, small and pretty, while the mother had orange hair that stuck out, and a heavily painted face. She graciously told me, "I will allow you some time to think about it." I was dumbfounded.

A few days later I told them I wasn't ready for such a commitment at this time, and, in any case, I had a girlfriend in Dublin. This was the beginning of the end of the whirlwind romance. My reluctance must have been humiliating for Nina. When she finally disappeared, I realized I was simply a concept to her and a substitute for the previous year's Irishman. The thought of marriage under the mother's supervision was unimaginable and ludicrous. I decided it would be a decision for next year's Irishman.

When Mervyn and I took the apartment, we didn't realize it was across the road from the Bluebird Bar that our growing circle of student friends would later frequent. We would typically arrive there after midnight when the piers closed. Unfortunately, some got the trick of going across the road to our apartment when they had enough drink. As time went on, I frequently came in to find my bed already occupied and I would head off to sleep on the beach along with many of the others. The sun would wake us around 10:00 a.m., at the latest. I would proceed to have a quick wash in the sea, breakfast in a café, and on to the pier for work. Such was the circle of life.

The owner's nephew, Ralph, came around to collect the takings a few times a day. I got on well with him and having hinted a few times, he said directly, "On account of the bad pay, most staff are on the take." It took me a while to absorb this shock. When I mentioned it to Mervyn, he told me that he had already started to take his share.

Having checked with some others, I decided, albeit reluctantly, I should not be the odd man out. However, there was one problem: the counter was tipped at the end of each game and the dimes slid down into locked boxes. Most of the others, like Mervyn, were on games where the minimum wager was a quarter, and the coins went straight into their cash pouches. While my helper and I initially devised a way to divert dimes on their way to the locked boxes, our returns were paltry.

We developed a more lucrative income stream where we sold some of the big stuffed dogs for $20 apiece while making it look like the customer had won when the pointer stopped. When men and their girlfriends showed interest, we would convert some of them into purchasers. As a bonus on our last shift on Labour Day, Ralph left the lock open on one of the coin boxes and made sure we saw it. "Enjoy your trip home, and thanks for staying until Labour Day."

Just before leaving Atlantic City, one of the local young women, Gail, hosted a twenty-first birthday party for me in her home. I didn't know till someone told me the next day that, though we hardly knew each other, she too had her eye on me. The party was notable for the amount of drink and pot consumed. The only time ever I indulged in pot was at that party, and for some reason, it didn't affect me. Maybe I wasn't sucking deep or often enough.

In any case, I reverted to drink as my sole vice and never looked back. In the early hours, Gail said the remaining guests could stay in a mixture of bedrooms and on couches. "You're coming with me," she said, as she dragged me up to her bedroom. I presume she had plans for me, but I was blind-drunk at this stage and immediately fell asleep. There is no better contraceptive than Arthur Guinness.

This trip was my first experience of America and was capped off when Mervyn and I borrowed a Volkswagen from a friend we made on the pier to drive to Tampa, Florida. We were going for the wedding of my friend Duncan to an American girl he had met the previous summer. We arrived miraculously on the morning of the wedding and had a quick swim in the Gulf of Mexico beforehand. The bride's family did not allow drink, so at the reception, they had a green-coloured concoction in honour of the Irish. We were mesmerized by the vast open spaces on the trip and the generosity of everyone we met. I was impressed by the general live-and-let-live attitude. Success was encouraged and celebrated as opposed to a prevalent begrudgery in Ireland at that time. It was exciting times, the year after Woodstock, and anti-Vietnam protests in full-flight. Students were very idealistic and waking up to the nastiness of their politics.

The magical summer was over, and while I enjoyed and benefited from the experience, I was looking forward to getting home to my girlfriend, Susan, and giving her the big stuffed dog I brought her from the pier.

28
FIRST LOVE

Susan and I first met at a hotel beach party on Barley Cove Beach, ten miles from Toormore, when Tom and I crashed after the pub closed in Crookhaven. I was friendly with Cathal, the pianist at the hotel, and he put me sitting beside her. In truth, through a mixture of the drink and the darkness, I didn't see her very clearly that night. However, my senses were alert enough to be smitten.

After that, a relationship grew slowly and we continued to meet in Dublin. She had shoulder-length fair hair, high eyebrows, and a small nose in a face that glowed with life and smiled easily. I had two golden years. She was finishing secondary school the first year, while I was in third year at university. I was now living on campus and used to look forward all week to her visits on Saturday. I would be at my window high up west of the Chapel, on the left side of the front square of Trinity College. She'd emerge from under the front gate portico and negotiate her way across the cobbles with her flowing black and white coat, graceful posture, and characteristic short-stepped walk.

When I was in my final year, I was ensconced in the renowned Botany Bay corner of the campus, sharing with my friend Alan. Oscar Wilde stayed in the building at one time. Susan had left school and was taking a secretarial course. She came to our rooms for lunch on a regular basis.

The next fall, having finished her secretarial work, she started at Trinity, and I started my first job as an engineer with the organization in charge of the telephone system. I knew something was wrong, but I could not put my finger on it. My jokes weren't as funny anymore. It took me a while to register that she wanted a break, at least for a while. While not overjoyed about this, I accepted her wish to become independent as she sampled university life for the first time.

That winter was difficult for me, with much recrimination and unhappiness. However, I eventually began to accept the situation and put a new life together. I had slowly begun to live again, had the beginnings of a new relationship, and if things had remained so I think I would have shortly fully re-joined the human fray.

Just home from work one sunny evening in April, I was listening to the radio and television before the six o'clock news, as was my custom. I saw the silhouette through the frosted glass panel in the door of the flat, encircled with the early evening sun. On opening, I had a rush of exhilaration. Susan was there, smiling and wearing her blue jacket, her natural fair hair as beautiful as always, her face radiant. We went out to a singing pub on the north side of Dublin that night; it was like nothing had changed, and we were in old times again.

We rebuilt our closeness and I was looking forward to a whole summer together in Dublin to solidify our relationship. And then, a month later, disaster struck. Her father was killed in a plane crash outside of London. Everything changed. The aftermath was horrific. Susan was devastated. I stayed at her home during the time of the funeral and did my best to support her through this difficult time, but things were never the same. She left me for the second, and last, time in September, and for a while I thought my life was over. I was not able to attend any social event where she was present, and because by then most of our friends were in common, that meant most events. I could not understand how I could be best friends with her, and then not able to see her at all.

I was bereft. I felt abandoned, empty, worthless and overwhelmingly lonely. I could see no joy in anything and no purpose ahead. I saw her everywhere on the street, in my daytime ruminations, and in my dreams. The void and the pain were of a level that I never experienced before or since. This was my first knowing encounter with depression, although I did not understand that at the time.

I slowly descended into a state of despair and anxiety such that I could not work effectively; I escaped to my parent's home in Toormore. After feeling sorry for myself for a while, I joined my friend Tom, the farmer, and worked with him daily to help regain some emotional stability. This worked to an extent because when one of my bosses called wondering would I like to come back, as there was a low-stress training course scheduled for the following week, I agreed. It was hard facing everyone on my return, but I did, and I slowly regained my strength. As well as thriving at work, I began to have a social life again.

Susan tried to reach out to help me when I returned to Dublin from my wandering in the wilderness. She visited me and I welcomed her cheerfully. She talked to my flat mate while I finished cooking my dinner in the kitchen as tears ran down into the pan. Unfortunately, her visit reminded me only of what I then knew I had lost, and lost forever. Reality had finally squashed my hope.

A long time afterwards I realized I'd put Susan on a pedestal and become too intense and dependent on her, in a needy way, and that my expectations were unrealistic. Also, I think I couldn't give her the support she needed at that time. Sadly, I did not have that insight at the time, but I presume these were some of the things that diminished her love and made her need to escape. Friends advised that, if there was to be any chance of her coming back, the best thing would be to act nonchalant. I managed to pull this off reluctantly after our first parting. However, while I understood the wisdom, the second time I was unable to act or pretend.

She was my first love, and while I eventually learned to love again, it took time and it was difficult to have the same feelings. She has always had a special place in my heart. This place is now blurred in history, over fifty years ago, and visited less and less. I tied up all her letters with a piece of string and stored them with a lock of hair she gave me to remember her.

29

YOU NEED NONE OF THAT HERE

My first day of work at the Department of Posts and Telegraphs in Dublin, the third of September, 1971, was my twenty-second birthday. I arrived full of idealism and energy as a newly graduated engineer, ready to set the world alight. What I did not realize was that the Department of Posts and Telegraphs was part of a government ministry that emerged from the old Telegraphs Department run by the army. As a result, it was one of the most autocratic, bureaucratic, and sclerotic of all the government ministries.

The section I joined was responsible for the installation and maintenance of all telephone exchanges in the greater Dublin area. At the time I joined we were responsible for thirty-two exchanges, twenty-eight of which required immediate expansion. This crisis had developed as a result of lack of resources, antiquated technology, and rapidly increasing demand. However, the department was processing expansions at a rate of two exchanges per year, which went a long way to explaining why the average citizen had to wait between six to twelve months to get a new phone.

When I met my new boss, Cyril, I learned he had been a football hero for Dublin in the fifties and now owned some racehorses. He was gaunt with a hunted look that may have come from an incident on the football field in an All-Ireland final, where, allegedly, his brother ran across the pitch and punched him for missing what would have been the winning goal against arch-rivals Kerry. He had light brown hair and a long thin nose and projected the air of an absent-minded professor. "You will get on great here, Bill, and the boys will take care of you," he said, and as I left his office, "Feel welcome to come in here any time."

My desk was in the corner of a large office that had two other incumbents—Joe, who I thought was old, was probably in his mid-thirties, and Bob, who I thought was very old, likely in his mid-forties. At lunch the first day Joe took me aside to give me some advice about getting on in the department. He pulled a sheaf of notes from his pocket and said he had been at a Dale Carnegie personal development course the evening before in the Shelbourne Hotel. He began to take me through lists of the characteristics required for success, such as initiative, drive, hard work, commitment, and the like. I was impressed.

"The first thing I am going to tell you is that you need none of that here," said Joe. "And the second thing I am going to tell you is that you can do nothing here if you like, but don't make a mistake."

"Your personal file," he went on, "will have two items now, your application, and your interview record. In a year, there should be a third piece of paper indicating that you have been promoted from Assistant to Executive Engineer. The only thing preventing this and future promotions would be if there was an extra piece of paper in the file documenting a screw-up."

I took these wise comments home to ponder. That's all I remember from my first day. Despite, or maybe because of, Joe's incisive views on the criteria for success, I came to like him over our many weeks together. He was a good-looking man with neat, greying hair that was a little greasy, presumably from not being a daily communicant with water, as was not uncommon in Ireland at the time. Overall, he had the mien of a man well serviced with the basics, and why wouldn't he, as he lived at home, in Drumcondra, with his mother. Joe took all his vacation time in half and single days. He would call up the office in the morning and say he was taking off to go to the horse races. Depending on how well he did at the horses, he might then go to the dog races in the evening at Shelbourne Park. Sometimes after one of these forays to the horses, he would invite his girlfriend to meet him for drinks at Powers Hotel, in the city centre, before heading off to the dogs. They would return to Powers for more drinks after the dogs, before she took the bus back to her flat in Rathmines, and he would take another bus back to his mother in Drumcondra. I had the impression that Joe rated the care from his mother above any fleeting pleasures of the flesh.

My other co-worker, Bob, furthered my education too on many fronts. He spoke with a reasonably cultured accent and was evidently a Renaissance man of the arts and *bon viveur*. He had an aura of self-confidence about every movement. He introduced me to "top drawer" work. He would, for example, be studying the novel *Ulysses* and two to three commentaries on the book at the same time. All of these he would have in the top drawer of his desk so that if anyone walked in, he could simply slip it shut. Bob was one of the most brilliant people

I have met. He would typically work flat-out on a project for a week, and in that time achieve what most of us would take double the time to do. He would then take a week studying James Joyce, or whatever other literary greats took his fancy, justifying the time no doubt on the fact that he didn't want to expose the lack of productivity of others.

At that time, Bob was the only one who knew how to operate and fix the new telephone-based talking clock. "Become an expert like me in something that makes you indispensable, in case the powers-that-be think of capriciously dispensing with your services," he impressed on me. "Look out for an opportunity and grab it," he advised.

As for me, I have no memory of doing any work of significance because I did not receive any relevant training, and my degree was useless in terms of yielding an understanding of the telecommunications sector. However, one day Cyril breezed into the office. "I want you to supervise the installation at the new Merrion telephone exchange, Bill," he said. "It's the engineer's job to give orders to the technicians and the technicians should always know who is boss. The technicians tend to dress well and you will need to dress the superior part of an engineer."

This air of superiority was going to be difficult to affect, as I had already realized that a top-down management style was not the best for me. The challenge of establishing credibility when I knew absolutely nothing about the technology was frightening. I was terrified, but I said nothing.

On my first day at the exchange, I took the chief technician, Christy, for coffee. Sure enough, Christy was wearing a smart sports coat and tie and looked the part of a man about town.

Emboldened by the fact that he came from my region in West Cork, I jumped early on to the matter that was troubling me. "I must confess I know nothing," I blurted, "but I am willing to learn if you are willing to teach me." While Christy was digesting this in some amazement, I followed up with some trepidation. "In return, I will keep your ass covered from the higher-ups."

"I'm surprised, Bill, that an engineer would admit to knowing nothing," he said with a laugh. He accepted the deal, and this was the beginning of a great relationship. Christy was a good teacher and I learned a lot about telephone switching technology. A few weeks before the end of the project, I was beginning to think they might have forgotten about me back at the head office, and this paranoia progressed to images of somebody new sitting at my desk. After I'd made several calls to Cyril, he eventually responded and suggested we meet for a coffee.

After we were settled at a table in a café on Baggot street, Cyril started, "I have received good reports about your work on the Merrion Exchange." We proceeded to talk about family, sport, politics, and all the problems of the world until finally, we came back to my situation. "I've been watching you, Bill," Cyril said, "and you seem to me the type who wants to succeed and get on."

While I stuttered a "yes," he continued, "Then if I were you, I would fuck off out of here." He finished this piece of strategic advice by saying the only thing keeping him from insanity was his interest in his racehorses.

Within two months I was gone to start a new career. However, I have always had warm feelings for those I met in the Department of Posts and Telegraphs, and for my early induction into the University of Life.

30

ACCOUNTANCY

Moving from the "*mañana*" level of urgency as an engineer at the Department of Posts and Telegraphs, to Arthur Andersen (AA) in Dublin, as an articled clerk, was a major culture shock. AA was the largest accountancy and consultancy firm in the world at that time and had been operational in Ireland for a few years, on the backs of American clients who had set up after the country joined the European Economic Community (EEC). I was not to know that this trickle of US companies would turn into a flood and become the basis for Ireland's subsequent economic strength. By fortuitous twists of politics and geography, Ireland became like a huge aircraft carrier for US companies, offshore to the EEC. The fact that the natives spoke English and were steeped in the tradition of touching forelock to a colonial power made the entry process reasonably smooth.

AA regarded itself as the crème de la crème of international auditors and charged fees accordingly, which put them outside the reach of typical small Irish companies. They also paid staff highly, and this included a good market rate to new articled clerks. As a result, I was the envy of some of my friends in the other large accounting firms who were on traditional articled clerk slave-labour rates. The offices were in an up-market building by the canal and were carpeted and furnished to the hilt.

None of us then would have had the slightest doubt about the company's bright future, representing the elite in worldwide accountancy. It must have been a major shock to my ex-colleagues decades later, when, starting in 2002, it became embroiled in the Enron scandal and collapsed like a house of cards.

Three of us joined in the summer of 1972—Cormac and Paul were business studies graduates from Trinity, and I was an engineering graduate. We started by spending five weeks in Manchester at a basic introductory accounting course, along with colleagues from the UK offices. We followed this with an immersive two-week Auditing course in Versailles at the management school there. While exhausting, it was exhilarating to be with some of the high achievers of Europe. The only breaks between breakfast and bed were playing indoor soccer some evenings. There was some vague news of Israeli athletes killed at the Berlin Olympics but we didn't have time to get the details or internalize the horror.

Frank, the managing partner in Dublin, told me later, "You know, Bill, you had the highest score from training courses of any previous Dublin employee."

This was good for my self-esteem, as I had worried whether I could compete without any previous knowledge of accounting. "A mind uncluttered from what is taught in business school can sometimes be an advantage," Frank said. "We have high hopes for you."

The first order of business when I returned to Dublin was my introduction to the time sheet. The increments were five minutes, and the whole day had to be attributed to client codes and a limited number of non-billable expense codes, two of which I was warned by my peers to use sparingly. The bosses viewed "managing library" and "general admin" with disfavour, as these were seen as cover for wasting time. The timesheets were mailed off weekly to the AA office in Milan to be processed by their computer—the only one owned by AA at that time in any of its European offices.

This immersion in US corporate culture at a relatively early age, although I resented some of it at the time, was very useful to me in my later career. I learned what a day's work was, and a key lesson was to recognize and thrive in a hard work environment, and be accountable.

31

BOMBS IN BELFAST

At that time, the majority of our clients were multinationals, all based outside of Dublin. We had to travel on our own time, so this often meant travelling on Sunday evening and returning late on Friday. Belfast, which was in the middle of what were euphemistically called "The Troubles," was an interesting special example. Our audit team travelled by train and didn't have to travel on its own time. The client was part of a large telecommunications multinational situated in Monkstown, in the middle of a Protestant area on the edge of Belfast.

One of our audit team who had been on the audit the previous year provided some briefing. "The client workers will be very upset if they know that we are from Dublin," he said. "Also, I heard that some Catholic consultants were strung up to the rafters on the shop floor recently, when their religion was disclosed," he said. He warned us not to venture on to the shop floor unaccompanied by management.

We stayed in the Europa Hotel that had the dubious record of being the most bombed hotel in the world. Journalists from the world's press were in the first-floor bar every evening, a *Time* magazine representative smoking a large cigar, and a journalist from the *New York Times* drinking double brandies.

The abundance of smoke and drink made it reminiscent of Hemingway's Havana before the revolution.

I, being the junior, drove the team in our hired car to and from the client premises at Monkstown, a few miles out along Belfast Lough.

"I will sit in the back so I will have a better chance of survival if we hit a bomb," said my boss, who was pompous with delusions of grandeur.

Armoured tanks were everywhere on the streets. It was unnerving at times when I ended up behind one of these at traffic lights. While it was stopped in front of us, there would be a gun pointing straight at us from a soldier at the back. However, like the locals, we got used to sharing the streets with these unusual companions.

AA's concession to danger was that we did not have to adhere to the standard daily allowance; we could eat as much as we wished at the Europa and charge it to the client. On reflection, given the profusion of cigars and drink, I think the journalists were getting a better deal. My boss regularly started dinner with steak tartare, and followed up with filet mignon for main course. When young, you don't think too much of these things and balance an extra steak on expenses against the risk of injury or death. One evening, a bus pulled up and was abandoned at the front of the hotel, directly below where we were eating at the front windows of the dining room. At that time hijacked buses were commonly used as delivery vehicles for bombs. Our response was to pick up our plates and move to the back of the restaurant. Luckily, there was no bomb that evening, and the food was good.

We were not allowed to date client women, and we were not to take the car out in the evening. I broke both rules. I figured if AA was prepared to pay no more than a good steak for danger money, I would take these strategic decisions myself. I took Mary Craig from the client company on a date and she guided me through the Falls and Shankhill, two of the most troubled areas, the former Catholic and the latter Protestant. We went up to the top of the Cave Hill, from where I was able to appreciate the beauty of Belfast spread out below. The inner city was directly beneath us. Across the lough to the left, where the Titanic was built, the cranes of the shipyards were like giant giraffes genuflecting in harmony; the multitude of blinking city lights evoked a slumbering peaceful giant, temporarily hiding the pockets of evil.

I was somewhat distracted, of course, by the beauty of my gracious date. Her first name would imply that she was Catholic, but her last name, Protestant. I never asked or knew.

32
IRISH TRADE BOARD

I went into accounting mainly on the influence of friends and because it was meant to be the coming thing, especially to be an engineer and an accountant. I was by now beginning to realize it was only the coming thing if that was what I wanted to do. I had applied for a marketing job in the Irish Trade Board, on a random advertisement I saw in a newspaper, that for me conjured up images of adventure and diving into swimming pools in Abu Dhabi. I was interviewed and had been accepted, but twice had asked for extensions to the decision date, as I could not make up my mind. The last extension was nearly over when I told my principal, Ronan, my predicament while on a job in Limerick. He had become a good friend and confidant. He knew me well enough to know that I was not ready for the discipline of more accountancy exams at this time and was a little disillusioned by the narrow scope of the profession. I did not have the motivation and ambition of most of my colleagues. It could have been because of the values of my early upbringing or the fact that I was not too influenced by the possibility of significant wealth. I could not make a decision and was swayed by whoever last entered my revolving door.

"Leave the open plan and go into one of the closed offices over there, call Frank and tell him you are leaving," said Ronan, referring to the managing partner.

"He will ask if you have written to accept the job yet and it is important you say yes," said Ronan, "otherwise he will ask you to take the train to Dublin, and he will talk you out of it."

I went in reluctantly to an empty office and could see Ronan in the open plan through the glass, as I called Dublin. I did as Ronan said, and when asked by Frank, pretended I had sent the letter of acceptance. "I am very sorry to hear this, I think you had a great future with the company," said Frank. "I would have asked you to come and talk if you had not committed."

On such procrastination, impulse, and peer pressure, I have stumbled into most of my life-changing moves. But by and large, this "scientific" method of decision-making has served me well. I left Arthur Andersen a few months later to join the Irish Trade Board.

I enjoyed a great start in a general marketing department and after a few months was selected to manage trade missions to the Middle East. This involved travelling in advance to Saudi Arabia, Kuwait, Bahrain, Abu Dhabi, and Dubai with my colleague, Paddy, from the Beirut office, to seek contacts for each participant. On my first mission preparatory visit, Paddy led the way in his excellent non-leadership style. I was intrigued by the new sights and sounds and by the graciousness of the Saudis. I avoided where possible the shots of Arabic coffee—it was bitter as hell—and settled for the small glasses of tea. The severe heat was also new and I got violently sick in Al Khobar towards the end of the trip. Paddy understood and made allowances for my newbie behavior. Over the years we built a great friendship.

Then I completed logistical arrangements and briefed each company back in Dublin before accompanying the trade mission. There was great excitement and buzz around these trade missions. At Jeddah Airport I managed to get our VIP, Ivor Kenny, head of the Irish Management Institute, and myself on a flight to Riyadh when we had no bookings and there was chaos around the check-in desk. Then I bluffed our way into a suite in our hotel in Riyadh by asking to put a gold medal present we had for a prince in the safe.

We moved on to Abu Dhabi where I remembered my earliest image of the Trade Board as I dived into a swimming pool. This first experience was in a hotel in the evening, looking out over the sea with the stars overhead. This was the life.

After organizing two trade missions to the Middle East within my first year, I was appointed to run the Glasgow office. I was stunned. I had thought my growing expertise in the Middle East would be best utilized in my present position. I did appreciate the joke in the organization that if you knew French, you would most likely be sent to Germany. While the Glasgow office would be a promotion, I could not reconcile to it, and in an environment where my contract obliged me to go wherever asked, I did not have the self-confidence to seek discussion with my boss. I realized that at core I was afraid to go and live on my own with none of the social supports I had built up in Dublin. Also, I could not get interested in my perception of Glasgow compared to what I was doing in the Middle East.

I spent most evenings in my flat ruminating over what seemed like an insoluble situation and always went to sleep and awakened without a solution. I became dysfunctional at work. I was depressed and anxious, and although my reaction was similar to when Susan left, I didn't fully recognize this at the time. Also, I did not think that mental health issues were legitimate and did not dare to raise them.

Finally, in desperation, I went to the HR person and tried to explain my situation. He was understanding and suggested I take a break in a nursing home outside of Dublin. After setting out reluctantly, I stopped my car just short of the home and made one last effort to psych myself back into the fray. After more than an hour of misery, I could not come up with a plan that I had confidence I would implement. I thought of all of my achievements to date but success now seemed long ago. Depression mixed with anxiety immobilized me and I was not able to think properly. I felt I had no option but to continue to the home, as I did not feel capable of taking care of myself. I started the car, went back onto the road, and checked in at the home. It was a very lonely experience.

I realized after a while that this home had no psychological or psychiatric services so, apart from giving me some anti-anxiety medication, I was left to my own devices. I played tennis with a teenage girl but with very little communication. She was in her own head and I was in mine. I felt so lost and lonely.

I will never forget my girlfriend at the time, Pamela, who visited me after her work, on a very long journey by bus. She had blonde hair over a pretty face and she bobbled her head in a characteristic way when she walked. We had many great times and she was very supportive through my ups and downs. There was nothing she wouldn't do for me and I also liked her whole family. I let her go partly because I hadn't fully recovered from Susan and was not ready for a new commitment. I did not want to prevent her meeting others. Also, at that time I was finally beginning to think about the possibility of my mental health issues cropping up again, and how I would expect a girlfriend to deal with this. I hoped she realized I was being honest and at that time had no choice. I didn't hang on until somebody else came along. I often thought of the hurt I caused Pamela and what life may have had in store if I had stayed with her.

My boss, Colm, and his wife Pat, visited and he told me to forget about Glasgow and get well. I felt very guilty but also relieved. I will never forget his compassion and kindness. Soon afterward I felt good enough to get back to work. HR guided me towards a psychiatrist, and for the first time, I heard a diagnosis of manic depressive. This is now more commonly called bipolar disorder. I was so ignorant of anything to do with it. The diagnosis didn't really have much effect on me; I still believed that the depression would never happen again and I didn't take the prescribed medication once I felt better.

Soon after returning to the office, I started a few years of productive and satisfying work and a social life. I was selected by a new boss to start a section to promote the export of services, such as engineering consultancy and architecture, mainly to the Middle East and Africa, and thus started one of the highlights of my professional life.

33

AVONDALE

While travelling in the Middle East and Africa, I shared a flat at Avondale, a large house near Blackrock, and enjoyed some of the best times of my life. I had two flat mates: Alan was a teacher and amateur diver, and Jim was in one of the large accounting firms and studying for his exams. I had been in school and university with Alan, and university with Jim, and had previously shared apartments with each at different times. We had gotten together for an apartment search, and after viewing many over several weeks, each was rejected by one or all of us. We were frustrated and tired of our quest and realized that we might need to split up. Then we found Avondale.

Avondale was a large house on Avoca Avenue, a tree-lined road with stately big houses; it was the only one divided into apartments. The avenue exuded wealth. The name was the same as the house of Charles Stewart Parnell, a famous Irish political figure of the late nineteenth century. Looking up at the building, there was an above ground basement and several wide, granite steps up to the front door and first floor.

The landlady showed us downstairs to the basement, which was for rent. A huge sitting and dining room with bay windows looked out on the large back garden. Off this room, there was a bathroom and a small, but adequate kitchen. There were three bedrooms and two more bathrooms. At the end of this tour, I said to the other two, "I don't care about you guys, I'm staying here." Luckily, they were similarly disposed and we did the deal with the landlady.

One of the reasons we three got on together was because, at an early stage, we decided to have our own frequently used dishes and saucepans so that nobody should touch the others' equipment. This system also showed to whom dirty dishes belonged; reminders could be issued if necessary. One of the great freedoms I experienced for the first, and probably last, time was the facility to leave my coffee mug anywhere and come home and find it untouched. We were very different personalities with many different interests, and apart from all of us being fairly laid-back and flexible, the solution to the dishwashing was core to keeping the peace.

The landlord and landlady, Ted and Jo, were very amenable and they encouraged getting to know the other tenants to have good relations in the house. Hugh and Patricia occupied the top floor apartment; he was a salesman and maverick bon vivant and she was a designer for a carpet company. Colm, a young priest who also did some media work, occupied a one-room bedsitter inside the front door. Ted and Jo lived on the ground floor. Ted was a well-known TV personality and political pundit and Jo was a housewife. We were happy to allow them use our large downstairs room for parties for their arts and political friends. All the tenants were invited too.

At one of these parties there were three Rolls Royces parked outside. These were owned by some of the captains of industry, journalism, and politics. This level of quality automobiles probably contributed to some delusions of grandeur on my part, and I bought a convertible Triumph Spitfire sports car from my friend Alan, who was leaving town. While it was on the lowest rung of sports car hierarchy it was sleek and jet black and I thought it should have been enough to capture a blonde whose hair would flow in the wind. Unfortunately, it didn't work for me, probably because the few candidates whom I encountered realized my approach was as inauthentic as their hair colour.

While we hosted many of our own parties over time, the ones I remember best were those held after the Irish Trade Board Christmas party. When the Christmas party wound down, the thrill-seekers would continue to our place. We would get a barrel of beer and rent extra glasses. We didn't have any food—who needed that? We had no rules and with no officialdom, people tended to let their hair down. I walked into a bathroom once to find two frolicking in the bathtub. But what happened in Avondale stayed in Avondale.

The last Christmas party had an unusual trajectory. I had told people at the Trade Board party that I was retiring this event and there would be no party this year. However, most took no notice and came back anyway. We had a barrel of beer for our own use but no extra glasses. The ingenuity of the patrons finding implements from which to drink knew no bounds. All saucepans were plied into use; cans of peas, beans, and soup were opened, emptied, and thrust into action; even flower vases and the bases of flowerpots were deployed. When I got up the next morning and began to clean up, I found some genius had borrowed the budgie's birdbath.

We were holding this budgie in trust for a colleague of mine who had moved to New York. I think the frequent ambient noise and Jim's fitness regime for him, that involved flights around the room, may have caused the budgie some stress. In any case, I came into the sitting-room one morning to see Jim lifting the budgie from the floor of the cage back to his perch whereupon the budgie fell off again. He repeated this exercise over and over, reminding me of a Monty Python skit. "Jim," I said, "the budgie is dead."

We lived in Avondale for five years and all three of us met our eventual wives while based there. Alan met Bernie through my friendship with her and her apartment mate. She was a great woman, positive and strong and a great influence on Jim and me, as well as on Alan. Jim was next to find his Susan and she also was a great asset to the apartment. She used to joke to me when I pored over the Sunday papers and looked over my half-glasses making it clear I was not to be disturbed. Alan was the first to get married and I was his best man. I still have photographs of the three musketeers at the top of the steps outside the front door on the morning of his wedding.

I met Christine in my last year at Avondale. Early in our courtship, I treated her to dinner at my place. I cooked a grilled pork chop, boiled potatoes, and a can of peas. I peeled the potato skins back into the saucepan, to save the washing. I don't think she was very impressed but was polite enough not to say so. She would have been even less impressed if she had known it would be a long time before I cooked for her again. I had been brought up at the end of the era where the Irish mammy did everything for her darling sons, and they expected no less of their wives.

Also, by that time, my sports car was in trouble, requiring constant fixes from my hole-in-the-wall mechanic who had kept previous cars in action with the mechanical equivalent of duct tape. Christine was not impressed by the car and she was not blonde. Maybe that took the pressure off me, and by then, I had learned to tell more of the truth more often. My time in Avondale came to an end when I bought a house in preparation for marriage. The house was a ticky-tack in the far-out jungle of the suburbs. I sure missed the life of restrained debauchery in Avondale but I knew it couldn't last forever, and a new chapter of my life was about to begin.

34

BEST MAN

My first experience as a best man was in my early twenties. It was for my best friend, Tom, the farmer near my home place in West Cork, Ireland. Tom had an old van with a mattress in the back that had a dual purpose. When he came home late from the pub, having dropped me at my home, he would park at the top of the field where his cows were grazing and avoid waking his father. He would also get extra sleep time in the morning by herding the cows for milking with the van rather than getting up in the house and having to walk up the field. The other purpose, of course, was in case he met a young lady in the pub who showed interest in availing herself of the facilities.

Giana, from London, served in Gabe's Bar in Ballydehob, a small nearby town. She was there for the summer and stayed in Gabe's quarters over the pub. At the end of the summer, a problem emerged. Gina needed accommodation for a week because Gabe had some other visitors arriving a week before her flight home. Needless to say, Tom chivalrously offered to keep her at his farmhouse. To make a long story longer, she never went home.

Over time, there was increasing pressure from Giana's mother that he make an honest woman of her. Tom called me at my office in Dublin one day. "Just to let you know, I'm planning to get married but it will be a low-key job in Windsor," he said. Windsor was along the Thames from London where Giana's mother and aunts lived. "There will be no need for a best man, Bill, and I don't need you there," he continued. Then I got a call less than a week beforehand. "Giana's mother has been wondering whether I have nobody who would stand up with me," Tom said. "I need you now, Bill."

The morning and day of the wedding were classics. Tom and I were in the back of an old Morris Minor chugging up the M1 from London. It was a beautiful sunny day, without a cloud in the sky. The car belonged to John and Noelle, two artists who had driven from Ballydehob the day before. John sported long hair and a scraggly beard with disparate pants and jacket, the latter looking like it had been used for painting. Noelle, whom I had never seen wearing a dress, was in a long flowing outfit. Tom was resplendent in country tweeds. We were the full complement of the groom's party.

Outside Windsor, Tom noticed some flower vendors on the side of the road and called an abrupt stop to the Morris Minor. We all purchased boutonnieres. The church was one of those small, old, beautiful ones for which England is renowned, all wooden rafters and panels inside. Rehearsal of the best man's role beforehand consisted of Tom saying: "I'll call when I need you and step back when I tell you." The service was short.

The reception was held in Giana's aunt's garden, genteel with its mix of exotic flowers. Some of her pretty young cousins sported exotic names, as they flitted around like butterflies in scant flowery dresses.

The small group started to drink, everyone standing up at the beginning. Then as the sun began to sink, most sat on chairs and the grass, and finally at dusk, many were horizontal on the ground. I still have faded photos showing this progression of conviviality.

The final act in this great wedding was when Tom and Giana got ready to depart in his trusty old van. John, the artist, had painted in the horizontal side panel a recognizable image of coitus. The image was impressionistic enough that some of the nice people were able to pretend they didn't notice, as the couple departed. It was probably the most enjoyable of all the weddings I have attended because of the informality and simplicity of events. Also, I was so happy for Tom that he had found a soulmate. Over time they built a very successful integrated farm and food empire.

My brother, Rich, married Mary in Cork. At that time, a Protestant marrying a Catholic had to swear and sign to bring up any children as Catholic. Rich wouldn't do this and booked an audience with the notoriously tough Catholic bishop, Connie Lucy. The bishop was very gracious and said, "You are the first Protestant to come to see me about this in many years." After a long chat about sport and affairs of the world, the bishop said: "I suspect from talking to you, no matter what I say, you will follow your own counsel."

"I wouldn't put it quite like that," said my surprised brother, and after that, he never heard another word. I was best man and the reception was in the Grand Hotel, Crosshaven, a seaside town outside of Cork.

Alan, from Avondale, and Bernie were next up. When it came to marriage and best man, Alan chose me, as I had known him through school and university. They were married in the chapel at Trinity College, which apart from being a great setting, was non-denominational and so satisfied all sides. It was a memorable occasion in the grandeur of the Trinity chapel with a reception afterwards beside Killiney beach.

I was best man at three more weddings in Dublin—Alan, my school friend and roommate at Trinity; Jim, flat mate from Avondale; and David, from the Irish Trade Board. They were all memorable in their own way, and I was honoured to have been invited. Six times the best man may be a record. I think the reason why these six performances arose was a mixture of being the first choice a few times, but also a compromise candidate, sometimes a default choice, and being in the wrong place at the wrong time. My ability to remain calm, conciliate with some patience, and having no fear of giving a speech were possible additional factors.

35

MY WIFE

I met Christine for the first time when I was twelve years old and she was a few years younger. Her family came for holidays in my parent's rental cottage in Toormore. She looked cute with her brown hair parted on the right, held back in a clip on the left, and reaching to her shoulders. We played games together. She wore green shorts and I showed her how to use my pellet gun. She made an impression on me.

I didn't see her again until the spring of 1977 when I was twenty-seven and we were both in Dublin. I attended a field hockey game where some friends were involved and I met her in the company of a guy. We recognized each other and had a friendly conversation. She had the same hairstyle I liked, and an exquisite Protestant nose. It was slender and so straight you could cut butter with it, as distinct from my roaming Mediterranean version. She told me she worked for Aer Lingus. I wondered that evening whether the same spark I felt as a child would still be there. The next day I recounted the story to my friend, Olive, who sat at the next desk, as we both looked out on Sandymount Strand. I asked for her advice. She urged me to call Christine, ask her out, and satisfy my curiosity. I was not in the habit of calling girls blind like this and it took a while for me to pluck up the courage. I had two previous long-term relationships, one where I loved too much and one where I didn't love enough, and my confidence in reading and dealing with the female persuasion was at a low ebb.

I called her at her office at Aer Lingus and again she was very friendly and sounded glad I did. However, when I got round to asking her out, she responded,

"I'm seeing another guy." But she said this gracefully, with a tinge of remorse, and in a way that I did not feel embarrassed or put down. When I got off the phone, I turned to Olive, "Why the fuck is it the one time I had the courage, she's already spoken for?"

"Oh, don't worry, there are plenty more out there. Besides, maybe you could try her again sometime in the future," said Olive.

A few months later I returned from a business trip to Libya. My friend Ian, who had been with me at the hockey game, called me. "I saw Christine's boyfriend at a recent game but he was on his own. Also, I forgot to tell you last time, I know him and he is a thundering bollocks. Try again." I needed no further encouragement and was on the phone the next day.

This time, she agreed to a date, and I shouted "Hurrah" to Olive as I put down the phone. We had a pleasant, few hours at The Old Stand Pub mainly reminiscing about our families and mutual friends and what we had been doing since our collaboration with the pellet gun. I thought it would be premature to mention my previous feelings at this time.

I booked a second date as I delivered her home. A week later I was at a charity reception with a friend without whom I would never have attended. Christine was also there with a friend without whom she would not have attended. I didn't see her until she came up to me as I was leaving. Our date was scheduled for a few days later, she reminded me, and in truth, if I hadn't met her then, there was a good chance that I would have chickened out.

The second date in O'Neill's Pub went well and so did the subsequent ones. There was one incident early that summer that earned me some points. Late on a Friday afternoon with the sun shining, she called me in a very upset state: "I've had a bad toothache for days. My dentist has tried to extract it and failed and I can't get hold of him now. I don't know what to do," she said. I went to collect her and took her to my dentist, Eddie Cotter, an eccentric Corkman with whom I had a good relationship. As was my custom, I walked right into his clinic in an old Victorian house on Morehampton Road. "Hello, Eddie, can I ask you a favour?" I said. Turning from his unsuspecting open-mouthed patient in the chair, "Ah, hello Bill, I suppose you have some Danish pornography for me after your travels," he said. He could see by my face I wasn't in the mood for our usual joking, so when he heard my story, he agreed to look at the problem after he had dispatched this last patient. He stayed late, sent me to the local pharmacy to get some extra strong anesthetic, extracted the offending tooth, and ended the problem. "I really appreciated that," she said and I saw the relief on her face. I knew I had scored points.

We went for many picnics up the Dublin mountains that rose in a great rounded hump guarding the south side of the city. As we went higher, the vegetation was sparse, there were few people, and we'd lay out a rug on a grass patch beside the narrow road. Christine was mainly responsible for the food. I was introduced to delicacies like cheese, croissants, and white wine and napkins; she had already begun to civilize my eating habits. We also did a camping weekend in Galway, all in that open sports car. She always dressed in style, usually wearing an accessory to complete the look.

Later in the summer, I went on a holiday with a friend to Torremolinos in Spain. While there, he met an American girl who subsequently became his wife. I wasn't really in the mood to join the meat market anymore, and to divert myself from the scene I started to write down my thoughts on Christine and myself in a diary-like format that finished up as a long love letter. I realized she was the one for me. We had so much in common, such as coming from the same county and having the same religion; the latter was not important to us but mattered to our families. Also, she had a calm demeanor, low tolerance for bullshit, and was very careful, all of which was the opposite to me. And, of course, she was hot. I wrote in a regular-sized copybook and eventually filled over fifty pages essentially making the case for why she should marry me. I was twenty-seven years old when I gave her the book.

Sometime in the fall, she agreed to marriage. We went to buy the engagement ring and what she chose was well over what I could afford but I didn't want to be a cheapskate. Also, I hoped this was forever. As we moved through Christmas, Christine and her mother made preparations for the wedding. I was keen to do it on St. Patrick's Day, so I would easily remember the anniversary. We had to settle for the day after because none of the churches did weddings on the holiday. An interesting sequel to this is that I sometimes remembered St. Patrick's Day rather than the anniversary. At one point, the idea was floated that men in the wedding party would wear tuxedoes. I managed to quash this both from my preference to get married in my own suit and the fact that my father had never worn one in his life and was unlikely to do so now. As a matter of fact, I still have that suit but it doesn't fit anymore.

The wedding was in Carrigaline, Christine's hometown outside of Cork. She had a gorgeous dress, a band of small flowers on her hair, and looked calm and beautiful as she arrived at the altar steps. My uncle Mike, who was a cleric, officiated at the ceremony and Christine told me afterwards that he included "obey" in the vows of "love, honour and obey," even though she had asked him explicitly to exclude it. Mike was from a different era where they believed in the importance of that prescriptive tradition. If he'd only known her, he would realize there was no chance she would obey me, or anyone else, for that matter.

The reception was in the Grand Hotel, Crosshaven, a few miles from Carrigaline, where, coincidentally, my brother had had his wedding reception a year previously. The hotel was an old Edwardian edifice on the side of a hill looking out over the bay, where there were yachts scattered in the harbor. At the event was the usual entertaining mix of rural and urban folk. Some were more inebriated than others and some took license from the occasion to get away with harassing those from the other family. An older man who was small and Mediterranean-looking specialized in dancing with tall women and frequently rested his head on their bosoms without receiving permission, never mind encouragement. Guests had a good time and I think my parents were proud to get the last of us married off safely. We had an official going-away, as was the custom. However, we had secretly booked into the hotel, and having driven off, turned around and entered the hotel again through a back entrance. Most of our friends stayed over, so we surprised everyone by appearing for breakfast the next morning for a more leisurely goodbye.

As we left the hotel, I began to sort out my thoughts. We had not been alone together for some frenetic days. I had a sense of how lucky I was to have Christine as a life partner and looked forward to our commitment to "in sickness and in health." She had a shining serenity that surrounded and protected me.

Yet, the honeymoon did not work out as planned. Christine had received free tickets to Tel Aviv from El Al. At her junior level in Aer Lingus, this was the only airline that offered her free flights. I looked forward to the trip as I had by then travelled in the Arab world and was keen to hear and see the Israeli version of events. Also, it would be special to visit some of the holy places of no less than three of the world's major religions. However, the Aer Lingus staff went on strike before the wedding and all travel perks were stopped. Christine's mother procured a friend's cottage for us in County Clare for a week, so we started married life, not beside the warm Sea of Galilee, but on the cold, cold shores of Lough Derg. A pleasant bonus was that for a second week we spent some time with both our families.

Christine eventually went back to work, not before suffering pneumonia from doing duty on the picket line. However, we finally got a break; she got better, the strike finished, and she was able to resurrect the El Al offer. We got to stay by the Sea of Galilee at last.

36

ISRAEL IS REAL

I had to get a second passport because many of the Arab countries at that time would not allow entry if they saw an Israeli visa. The same was true for South Africa for entry to African countries. I felt sad that any country had to suffer the indignity of having to accept a separate passport from citizens of other countries. We flew to Tel Aviv in July and stayed initially in the Sheraton, again courtesy of an Aer Lingus deep discount. We spent a few days on the beach and everything seemed very western with young women competing to see who could wear less and young jocks parading around showing off their undercarriages and Tarzan-like torsos.

I got talking to one of these who wasn't in the macho league. Later we went to a nearby café, and after he gave me guidelines to the country and the local scene, we eventually got into politics. He was not in favour of the governments' more draconian measures with the Palestinians. However, he was reasonably happy with the status quo. He admitted that he had never met a Palestinian, had never visited their places, and so found it hard to visualize improvement in their situation. He was very interested in Ireland. "Tell me about the violence in Ireland," he said. "How could you live in such a dangerous environment?"

What was happening primarily in Belfast he envisioned was widespread throughout the island. "How could you live in Tel Aviv, where unannounced bombs are a frequent occurrence?" I responded.

"Why not?" he retorted. It was an interesting insight for me that both of us perceived the other's place as dangerous, but not our own. Your home is where you live, no matter what.

Christine got so violently ill that she wouldn't chance leaving the hotel room at one stage. We were booked into a hotel at the Sea of Galilee, so I had to rent a car to transport the patient and walk by the lake on my own. This was my first exposure to a place made famous in the Bible where Jesus allegedly multiplied the loaves and fishes for a feast. It felt surreal, for this was a place I had heard of so often in my childhood, generating so many exalted images, and here it was in all its mundanity—perfectly ordinary and not even beautiful.

Christine was better by the time we headed for the Dead Sea. Since I had no expectation of what to see, I was less surprised to find it a bit of a non-event. The level was way down and decreasing rapidly because of the diminution of the River Jordan, which feeds it. The Israelis and Palestinians had been over-using the river upstream for fresh water and irrigation. There didn't seem to be any awareness then that, unchecked, there would be a crisis in supply just like the situation with the Colorado River and California.

At the time of our visit the heat was over 40 degrees Celsius, but there was no way I would not get in for a swim. I wanted to test the contention that because of the salt level the buoyancy was increased such that you could float unimpeded. Well, I validated that quickly. In fact, I was able to sit up and still not sink. There was somebody next to me reading a book. That was the fun part.

The water was dirty, maybe from too many people like me abusing it. Also, the salt content assailed any part of the body that was even slightly tender—in my case I discovered it was around my asshole. It stung coming out of the water and after I'd passed through a cold-water shower on the bank, it still stung. We made a hasty retreat resolving not to put this scourge on our bucket list again.

The most memorable moment for me was coming over the top of the Mount of Olives and seeing the East Gate and walled city of Jerusalem in the valley before us. There was the Dome of the Rock sparkling in the heat and the city spread out behind it. It was magical and met all my expectations. We checked into the Holiday Inn Mount of Olives. It boggled my mind that the much-storied Mount of Olives, a sacred place two thousand years ago, could have its name sullied by ties to a western God of Mammon. We came out next morning to meet three Palestinian children on camels offering tours of the city—Jewish, Muslim, or Christian. It was hilarious to watch this à la carte tourism and be assured youth entrepreneurism was alive and well.

We drove out to Bethlehem to see Jesus's birthplace. It was thronged with tourists. The alleged birthplace was at a marble slab with a church built over it. Several strands of Christianity had their own churches there—Armenian, Eastern Orthodox, Greek Orthodox, Catholic. I was reminded of the truism that

Jesus could not be responsible for all those who agreed with him.

Our last stop in Jerusalem was at the Via Dolorosa, where Jesus was reputed to have walked to his crucifixion. It was a beautiful street, too narrow for cars and still cobbled. As I was lost in a reverie comparing again to my childhood dreams, I was interrupted by two youths emerging from a side alley and whispering, "Master, like to sell blood?" I would have been tempted but Christine intervened—she had heard stories that in places like this you couldn't be sure they wouldn't take all eight pints. I politely demurred and got back to my reveries.

We returned to Tel Aviv at the end of our trip, where something unusual and thrilling happened. I was changing traveler's cheques into cash at the reception desk in the Sheraton, when the young woman told me there was someone at the Hertz desk with the same name as me. I didn't believe it because many people mistake the spelling and pronunciation. In any case, I went over and sure enough the young woman there had the same name—Sharon Jermyn. She was South African and also carried an Irish passport. She told me about her background; her father was Irish, left to join the British Navy, and settled in South Africa after the war. The intriguing thing for me is that he came from a family of Jermyns in Ballydehob, West Cork, which is a few miles from where I grew up and where my great grandfather came from. From other things she said, I think her mother was Jewish and the father was obviously a pragmatic Irishman who'd acquired Irish passports for the whole family. My mind boggled at the coincidence of us meeting so far from home. I had never met an unknown Jermyn, even in Ireland. We promised to keep in touch.

This was a great trip where I experienced the great religious sights, received a sore ass in the Dead Sea, and finally met my previously hidden South African cousins. I bought a T-shirt on my last day that proclaimed "Israel Is real". It expressed one of the basics of this troubled region.

37

SPECIAL BOSS

Sean, assistant chief executive at the time, said he would take me on soon after I returned to work after my depression. He had a project in mind. He gave me responsibility to develop a new section to promote the export of services for the first time. The majority of our initial clients were construction professionals—architects and consulting engineers. Later we became involved with airline services, medical and educational services, and a range of government-to-government expertise. Also, we had to get to know our way around Brussels because Ireland had recently joined the EEC and was involved in short-listing construction professionals for projects it was funding in the developing world, primarily in Africa.

One of the first things I became aware of was that I never had to prepare or review a budget. Sean took care of that and also of feeding the system with targets and operational progress statistics. I never remember him giving me a direct 'do-that' kind of order; his style was to question and discuss, and he trusted that I would usually come to agreement. He also regularly discussed other issues he was working on and sought my views. He made me feel important and I tried to be objective.

Sean had great vision and organizational skills to match. He once put together a high-level team for a visit to Saudi Arabia on a one-week deadline. Nobody else would have thought it possible, never mind have the energy and audacity to do it. We left London on Saudi Airlines. At that time, while liquor was banned, it was common to bring your own brown-papered-bag supply and the hostesses would turn a blind eye, while providing the mixers. Luckily, I had recently stopped drinking on planes because of its accelerated effects, and as we descended the stairs out of economy at the back, I noticed a fleet of black cars and people waiting around the first-class stairs at the front. I figured they were waiting for us and expected we would be travelling first class. I didn't know what to do, and in a panic led our team around the back of the plane, up the blind side, around the front, and began to filter into the group of Saudis. I'm sure they weren't fooled but at least they didn't see us coming out of economy.

On the plane, Sean had explained to the others, who had never been to Saudi: "All kinds of guys will be trying to hang on to your arms for taxis, or to peddle their wares." As we talked on the tarmac, a Saudi tugged on Sean from behind, to which he promptly responded by swinging his arm around and accidentally hitting him a wallop. The Saudi brushed it off and we were taken to the hotel without further incident. The next morning, the delegation turned up for the first meeting at the ministry. There was a long narrow conference table with a number of Saudis already in place. Sean was seated at one end beside the minister's chair, whom we awaited. The minister arrived, finally, in his flowing *thawb* (cloak). He took his place beside Sean and lifted his *keffiyeh* (headcover) back off both sides of his face. I recognized with horror that he was the one that received the benefit of Seamus's backhander the night before at the airport. Discussions went on for a few days and I cannot be sure what went wrong, as I was not directly involved. We did not win the contract. My guess is that we were out of our depth, and that was reinforced by the manner of our arrival. But full marks to Sean for trying.

My first venture to Africa was a five-week research visit to five countries, with particular reference to the prospects on EEC-funded projects. This was quite the project for someone with my limited experience, and I suspect Sean saw I was a little nervous. The day before I left, he called me into his office and told me: "I want you to know that if at any time during this trip you feel like coming home, you should do so, and I will not ask you why." I knew this was a genuine human gesture, but I wondered if he also realized the motivating effect—who would want to have to take up that offer?

My trip included Zambia, Kenya, Tanzania, Malawi, and Sudan and, apart from the work side, provided me with some unique personal experiences.

On my return, all I had to do was write up my report and take off for vacation in Corfu. That summer there was glorious weather in Dublin. One of my senior colleagues who had an office was away on vacation and so I took up occupancy. The week was so hot, I got into the habit of taking off my shirt, and when venturing into the open plan, I put on my tie and jacket again. I believe a few people were amused by this unconventional use of my tie—the badge of the trade. However, I could not leave well enough alone.

Going out for a late lunch one day, when I got to the carpark, I took off my jacket again and drove off in my open sports car. I was going up the ramp to the main road in my bare torso, albeit modified with a tie, when slowly turning in beside me was a carload of assistant chief executives who didn't look too amused. I knew I was in trouble and after I returned from lunch, Sean gave me the speech: "You know you are getting on well now, Bill, you don't want to ruin everything. It isn't as if I mind but some of my colleagues are a little more conservative."

It was clear to me he had taken some shots on my behalf. I kept my shirt on after that, although I could never see why it was so important as long as I was brandishing the tie as badge of the trade. I was a little high and everything seemed possible, but obviously did not recognize that then. Sean did, and came through for me.

AFRICA

38

EMBERS OF EMPIRE

My first stop on my first trip to Africa, was Lusaka, Zambia. My objective was to assess the prospects and opportunities for Irish consulting engineers and architects who were recently eligible for EEC-funded projects.

Mike and I became good friends when we met for the first time at Trinity College, Dublin in the fall of 1967. We were both studying engineering, had come from the same part of rural Ireland, and had a lot in common in terms of our outlook on life. This was the time of student revolt against the war in Vietnam, Maoist groups on campus, and the reigniting of republican activity in Northern Ireland. Mike was active in some left-wing groups and was always trying to convince me to join. I held back. While I was sympathetic to most of these causes, I was wary of the dangers of extreme '-isms,' especially nationalism. Despite my allergy to commitment, I was accepted and participated in two of the main activities of these groups—drinking and debating, although more of the former, I have to admit.

After graduation in 1971, Mike and I went our separate ways. When I heard he had moved to Africa with an Irish engineering company, I thought I would never see him again.

However, a few years and jobs down the road I ended up planning this business trip to a number of African countries, the first stop being Lusaka, Zambia. The year was 1975 and to my great joy this was where Mike was now living, and I looked forward to catching up on what seemed to be a huge time gap, although it was no more than four years.

We met at the bar of the Lusaka rugby club, one of the remaining bastions of white influence. It was like we had never parted—the immediate rapport, catching up on mutual friends, and picking up our common interests. However, when I asked him what life was like in Zambia, I sensed he was disturbed about something. Knowing that all the expatriates had servants, when I began to joke with him about this, he erupted, "You know, Bill, I would never have wanted servants."

"Well, then why do you have them?" I asked.

"When I told this to my new expatriate friends here, they laughed," he said.

He told me one of them said he had to have servants if he wanted to help these people and his employment will sustain a whole family living at the bottom of his garden. On pondering this logic, Mike said he responded by saying if he accepted this, he would at least pay them a proper wage.

Another of his friends addressed this by saying he would need to be careful about that as he could upset the applecart for everyone, and give his servants false expectations for future employment. Not liking where this argument was going, Mike said he made a final attempt to relate to the world he knew by asserting that he would at least treat them as equals. Yet another responded by saying he would need to be careful about this too as they would take advantage of him, and before he knew it, the cook would be stealing food for his family.

Mike realized that the post-colonial white man maintained a way of life in Africa that would not easily change. The distance between equality with the white man and second-class citizenship for black people descended like the steps of a staircase. At every stage there was a logical argument why change was not desirable, or even feasible, and in fact did not benefit the servants and their families. I left Mike knowing he was grappling with his conscience about the appropriate relationship between the expatriate and the native. I, also, had no solution at that time.

A few days later, at a party at the Finnish Embassy in Dar es Salaam, Tanzania, I sat at a table under a large tree with John and Samantha, an English couple in their late fifties. They were complaining about the state of the Tanzanian economy and the diminished esprit de corps of the servants. "Finbar was in charge of the horse when she went lame yesterday," moaned Samantha. They also complained about the economy and quality of life in England, and realized they were trapped between two ways of living. They had come out from England thirty years previously, transferring to an English company with no intention of staying more than a few years after they had children.

However, as the children grew up, they deferred their departure in favour of the lifestyle and a commitment to themselves that they would go back when the kids needed secondary education. When the time arrived, they found that the company package included subsidizing public school boarding back in the UK. Samantha realized that this was a higher quality education (or at least higher on the social ladder) than they could afford if they relocated back to ticky-tack land outside of Birmingham whence they had come, not to mention the three-bed semidetached and no servants, to whom she had become well accustomed. So again, following the inexorable expatriate reasoning, they decided to stay. And since then, they could not come up with any good reason to go home before retirement.

Except, there was one other matter that was causing them significant grief and might ultimately drive them out—the government was putting a new railway line through their front garden. The Chinese were building it from Lusaka to Dar es Salaam when the World Bank or other countries would not. Unfortunately, of all places in this large country, the design took it through Samantha and John's front garden. They had spent over a year writing to the authorities to prevent this atrocity, including citing their thirty-year tenure in the country. All was to no avail.

"We had to endure watching Chinese men with their African servants violating our lovely garden that I spent years creating," said Samantha, as tears began to well.

"Do you know what I told them when I got the last refusal letter?" said John. "I just wrote back and said, 'Fuck you too.'" John, at last, had come to understand that the white man's influence in Africa was now limited, and a thirty-year stay had given him no extra rights.

During my trip, I visited five countries in five weeks and met expatriate communities in each. All were grappling with the death pangs and embers of the empire and were having difficulties with the outcomes. A week after I returned to Dublin, I attended a reception for a visiting Zambian minister held at Iveagh House, on Stephen's Green, the headquarters of the Irish Ministry of Foreign Affairs. It was the "parlour" of the nation, a beautiful old house donated by the Guinness family, who were ironically part of the gentry. Walking up the slow winding staircase I had a sense of deja vu, although I had not been there before. On entering the grand reception room, I was approached by a flunky in white jacket and white gloves, brandishing drinks on a large silver platter. I looked up to the ceiling, expecting to see a large fan in slow motion.

There was no fan, of course, but otherwise I realized I had been at similar receptions in exactly similar rooms with fans, and staff wearing the same subservient gear, in each of the previous weeks. I wondered whether, although Ireland was the first to leave the empire, could it be one of the last to let go of some of the ingrained colonial attitudes and habits?

Irish people in general feel good about their lack of a colonial track record. However, the brutal performance of many Irish individuals in the service of the British leads me to believe that lack of opportunity rather than moral rectitude was the reason.

Although I didn't know it then, by temperament and circumstances I was an outsider and my worldview was broadening and changing. After I got to know more Africans and Arabs, I became more of an "outsider" in the white man's world, and to this day I support the underdogs and use every opportunity to stick pins in the hubris of the West and its delusion of being at the centre of the world.

39

EAST AFRICAN ODYSSEY

"You can check your bags through to Nairobi, sir," said the friendly young Sudanese woman at the check-in desk for Ethiopian Airways. It was 5:00 a.m. at Khartoum Airport after I had checked out of the Khartoum Hilton. I was still half asleep from going to bed late the night before.

I was twenty-four years old and travelling in Africa for the Irish Trade Board promoting Irish construction services companies and had spent a week in the Khartoum Hilton. A musical group was on a month's contract from London and they looked like they had been overeating to compensate for their limited talent. That night, like most nights, I had sat on my own among a sprinkling of other guests in the bar, nursing a pint of beer, which cost the equivalent of about six pounds; I couldn't afford to get drunk. I felt so lonely, as I did in most of my solo trips overseas. I wondered why I was doing this.

At that time, the Hilton was the only western hotel in Khartoum. It looked out over the slow-moving Nile and was a short distance up-river from Omdurman, where Kitchener, the British General, and his army destroyed the native forces with brutality in the late nineteenth century. I could not but be aware of the contrast between the hotel and its guests and the local people who were very poor. It made me realize how privileged we were in Europe and made me uneasy about the disparity and frustrated by how little I could do about it. The Sudanese people were the most hospitable and warm people I met in my travels in Africa, and so the more I felt sad about their condition.

I was travelling through Addis Ababa in transit to Nairobi to continue my preparations for a small delegation of consulting engineers and architects from Ireland to follow in a few weeks. From long experience, I never checked my bag through a transiting airport as I had found it a sure recipe for loss, especially if a change of plane and flight number was involved, as in this case.

"I would like to just check my bag to Addis, please," I said to the check-in woman.

"Oh no, sir, do you not trust us? There will be no problem. We never lose bags."

Her gorgeous brown eyes sparkled with life, and in my dulled stupor I could not find it in me to disappoint her. "Ok, just one bag to Nairobi," I mumbled.

There was no problem with the flight and we had an uneventful trip. Having arrived in Addis, I sought out the check-in desk for Nairobi. After much moving of paper and checking, the staff person said, "We have a full flight to Nairobi, sir, but for some reason, we cannot find your booking. Also, we have no record of your bag."

I recoiled with horror and began to carry out some reconnaissance for my bag around the terminal. Addis Airport was like a zoo with old men sitting on their bundles, cocks in cages, goats on tight tethers, some women in burkas cooking on kerosene stoves, children screaming everywhere, but no sign of my bag anywhere. I found a quieter corner so I could think of a solution to my predicament.

I spotted an Ethiopian Airways staffer wandering through the chaos and approached him, "Can you help me, please?"

After I explained my situation, he motioned me to follow him. We marched out through the swing doors of the terminal onto the tarmac. We walked through the blistering heat until we arrived under the open hold of the recently-arrived plane from Khartoum. He gave me a leg up into the hold and I proceeded to search through a jumble of bags. Just as I realized that my bag was not there, I heard a commotion on the tarmac below and another staffer, out of breath rushing from the terminal, called out, "Mr. Jermyn, we have found you a seat on the flight to Nairobi, you need to hurry."

The choice for me to go to Nairobi without a bag, or stay in Addis to try to find it was easy. Nairobi at that time had some similarities to a European city, while Addis had little to commend it. On arrival at Nairobi airport, I went to the Ethiopian Airways desk and reported my missing bag. When asked to list the contents, I included as many expensive clothes as I could think of.

I spent three glorious days in Nairobi with a change of shirt, underwear, socks, and toothbrush, all purchased with the few dollars given to me by Ethiopian Airways, and carried cavalierly in a plastic bag. While, as I said, Nairobi had many features of the "developed" world, it also had an underbelly of shame. The roads and streets were littered with people begging, not ordinary people but those with horrific malformations. I was told that the majority of these cases were a result of congenital syphilis.

Back at the airport, I was heading for Dar es Salaam and had been wondering would I have the courage to leave home next time with such minimal possessions, as I had been getting on perfectly well. On a whim, I diverted to the Ethiopian Airways desk to check whether there was any news of my possessions. I was pleasantly surprised to see my characteristic tartan bag standing there defiant and alone.

"Please open your bag, sir," said the Ethiopian staffer. She wanted to check that all the belongings I had listed in my lost baggage claim were present.

"I'm sure it's ok," I said and went to grab my bag.

"No, no sir, we must ensure everything is still there," she said, as she proceeded to lift the clasps and flipped the top open. The smell of dirty shirts and socks was overwhelming, and she recoiled in horror. I was able to charge all laundry to expenses, and so I always left home with as many dirty clothes as possible. Holding the claim sheet in one hand, she rummaged quickly with the other, and then looking up at me sadly said, "It seems we have lost your three mohair suits, sir."

I looked at her, smiled, and said, "Look, you have been such good people to find my bag, I am so happy. Why don't we call it quits?"

She smiled knowingly and graciously said no more.

40

BIAFRA

"That will be 8,000 Naira," said the receptionist at White's Hotel, as she reached for a key behind the desk. I gave her the cash.

"I will show you to your room," she said, and led me out to a dark courtyard that was surrounded by low buildings on all sides. The heat and humidity were overpowering. She opened a door and moved to turn on the light. "No need," I quickly retorted, "I prefer the dark." She shrugged her shoulders and disappeared quickly. There was no welcoming noise of an air conditioner as I groped my way in. I removed my alarm clock from the side pocket of my bag; it was past 2:00 a.m.; I set it for 5:00 a.m. and threw myself, fully clothed, on to the bed. I hoped sleep would overtake me before something else in the room did.

This was Enugu, capital of the state of Benin in Nigeria, in the mid-seventies. A few years previously there had been a horrendous famine in this region that was then called the Republic of Biafra. The famine was caused by a blockade by the Nigerian government as Biafra tried to break away, sparking a nasty civil war. Its plight became known internationally and attracted assistance from all over the world. The Biafrans eventually surrendered. The post-war and famine devastation was apparent everywhere, from the abandoned buildings to the hungry children on the streets.

Earlier that afternoon, I had arrived at Enugu Airport exhausted after a river trip into the jungle to inspect a new water supply development by my engineering client from Ireland. The client and I started our journey up-river in a small motorboat for more than an hour, and then, as the river got narrower and shallower, the boatman transferred us to a large hollowed-out log propelled by the boatman with a long pole. Soon the river became heavily crowded with dense undergrowth to the point where the foliage from each side met overhead in places.

Finally, with no warning, we emerged into a clearing on the left bank and the village that was the reason for our visit. All the houses were clustered together like a toy building set spilt from its box. They were constructed from wooden supports on which hung strips of foliage. There were a number of open fires around the clearing in front. Crowds of scantily clad children milled around us and our log boat. The adults were extremely hospitable. I was offered a greenish drink; I had no idea what it was, but I took my chances. The visit was a strange but exhilarating experience. The villager's reaction suggested that they did not often meet a white man, and it was my first experience of a black village.

Back at the airport, I looked forward to returning to Lagos to have a shower and a change of clothes. The first sign of trouble was when a voice came over the speaker: "Flight 856 has been delayed."

No more information, as was normal at Nigerian airports. I should have taken action. Hours later the speaker crackled to life again: "Flight 856 has been delayed, but for those who wish to hang around, it may go later."

I have never ceased to be amused by the Nigerian use of English. Like many ex-colonies, including Ireland and Jamaica, when their local languages were suppressed, they had taken English and made it their own.

There was only one half-decent hotel in Enugu, and it was usually full. I had checked out early that morning, on my way to the river trip, having had to heavily bribe to get a room the night before. Bribes, or dash, as they were called, were necessary for every imaginable function. On hearing the announcement, several people who knew the accommodation situation rushed to leave the airport in the hope of grabbing one of the few remaining available rooms. My better judgment said go, but my exhaustion tempted me to stay and gamble that the flight would eventually take off.

I made a bad gamble. I watched workmen buzzing around the plane on the tarmac when, about midnight, all the lights slowly went out. "The flight will not go tonight," the speaker announced. "It will fly again at 7:00 a.m."

There was a mad dash by the remaining hopefuls for the exit and waiting taxis. I got the fourth or fifth taxi, and realizing that the hotel would be fully booked, an alternative was needed. "Take me straight to the third or fourth rated hotel," I told the driver. That is how I ended up at White's Hotel.

I awoke in a daze to the ringing of my alarm and a pain in my head. It was still dark, but with the first glimmers of light I was able to take in a small and dirty room with multi-coloured geckos scrambling all over the walls, and strange insects crawling along the bed frame above my head. I struggled up, and seeing no washing facilities in the room, I opened the door to the courtyard. Through the faint light and bleary eyes, I was able to make out two doors on the other side of the yard. Not knowing what to expect, I stumbled towards them. There on one of the doors was a notice, on White's Hotel-headed notepaper: "Guests are kindly requested not to urinate in the bathroom."

Still groggy with sleep, I grappled with the significance of this polite request as I pushed open the door. The small room had a large hole in the ground and a wooden barrel full of water. Still puzzled, I opened the other door to find there was a similar hole in the ground but no barrel of water. I slowly began to grasp how, in this set-up, I could easily mix up the toilet and the bathroom, and hence the desist notice for urination in the latter. I couldn't resist, I took that notice and it is still one of my favourite pieces of memorabilia. The facilities reminded me of growing up in Toormore.

41
FULL CIRCLE

Tradition in Ireland dictated that the oldest son inherited the farm. If there were spare resources, another farm would be purchased for the second son. The third son (or second, if there was no farm for him) would be sent to the priesthood. This pre-supposed a level of resources that could not be met by the poorest class. The mother would be the main influencer of this career choice. She was usually a true Catholic believer. Often marriage had not met even her lowest expectations, and she was not fulfilled in her work. However, Catholicism was a suitable vehicle to maintain a stoical response to the harshness of life. Reconciliation to hard times and the promise of happiness in the next world were potent antidotes to her baby-manufacturing role. The consecration of a priest brought great honour and status to the family. It validated the mother with her peers and receiving communion for the first time from her son was a life-crowning achievement.

On the female side of the family, the career options were similarly limited. At least one daughter was expected to become a nun, and several of the others went into nursing if they were not already married off with good dowries for further breeding. There was not the same family prestige, however, attached to a nun as to a priest. As women, in general, were subservient to men, so were nuns to priests. Indeed, in many cases, they were almost like slaves to priests in the management structure.

Partly because of this process, the power and influence of the Catholic Church, and the limited alternative career opportunities, there was a large surfeit of priests in Ireland. Many were encouraged to go to the "Mission Fields" of Africa to show light to the heathens. In fact, Ireland could be said to have been one of the first countries to give bi-lateral aid to Africa—not of a material nature, but by influencing minds. In every small shop in rural Ireland, there was a charity box in a prominent place on the counter to support this crusade. As children, we were encouraged to give our pennies to the "Black Babies."

When I had the good fortune as a young man to travel extensively in Africa, I was shocked the first time I met a Nigerian who seemed to know nearly as much about Irish history as I did. He had learnt it in school at the feet of an Irish priest. Irish priests were all over English-speaking Africa and had worked their way into positions of influence. Kenneth Kaunda, the founder of Zambia, left his children in the care of his trusted friend, Father Walshe, when he was on the run in his pre-independence days.

Julius Nyerere, the charismatic president of Tanzania, relied heavily on an Irish priest for advice when he was going through his revolutionary period. In Nigeria, the Holy Ghost Fathers had become involved in politics. They backed the Biafran rebels in the early seventies and when the federal government put down the rebellion the priests were no longer welcome. Many of them decamped to Kenya. There are also numerous people in government and the private sector across English-speaking African countries, who received part of their education in Ireland.

On my travels, I met a number of these priests who did much good work that balanced some of the harmful aspects of their beliefs. After thirty, forty, and more years they had settled and were content in their new land and were then fearful of their return to Ireland, where they would miss their ministry and would face bureaucratic strictures they had long since left behind. Many of them had arrived shortly after their training at the Maynooth seminary still in their teens or early twenties, and totally ill-prepared for their new life in the bush. One priest in Nigeria told me how on his arrival in the Nigerian village he had been assigned to:

"The chief came to me at my welcoming banquet and offered me a young lady for my pleasure as a traditional sign of friendship."

This was an alien culture which Maynooth had not prepared him for. He had to sink or swim and learn to make his own judgments on important life decisions, not helped, but significantly hindered, by the comfortable doctrinal and hierarchical certainty with which he had been trained.

These priests were fearful of returning to Holy Ghost headquarters to serve out the remainder of their ministry under a restrictive structure that was now unpalatable to them. The culture they grew up in had all-but disappeared; the traditional way of extended family rural life had been replaced by the nuclear family, and machinery did most of the farm work. Ironically, many of the older practices still existed in their adopted African homes, but not anymore where they grew up.

They were also disappointed at the way the faith that had been so precious to them over the years had diminished in importance in what was a Catholic stronghold in their youth. Apart from being sickened by the pedophilia scandal, in general, the worldviews of these good priests had changed. As one said to me, "The church should be less concerned about pomp and power and more about compassion and collegiality." Also, many saw the enforced lack of significant participation of women to be unconscionable.

While these priests and nuns dutifully laboured in Africa over the years, the falloff in vocations in Ireland had been catastrophic, to the point that new entrants to seminaries were in low single digits. At the same time, Mass attendance by the Irish had also been decreasing. The shortage of priests, however, had been balanced by the arrival of young African priests, and waves of immigrants bolstered the congregations. Polish and African were predominant. The missionary effort in Africa had come full circle in the most unexpected way. The Irish took the faith to the Black "heathen," whose sons and grandsons returned the favour by coming to Ireland to preach to the new Irish "heathens" in their hour of need. The pennies to the "Black Babies" campaign turned out to be a good long-term investment and yielded a golden dividend for the Irish Catholic Church.

42

LIBYA PALACE

Tripoli in the mid-seventies was in full throttle with its oil boom, like the Robber Baron period in the US in the early part of the twentieth century, and in Moscow during the nineteen-nineties. It was the "wild west" where the rules were few, set by the strong, and the ordinary man had to live by his wits to survive.

Visiting there from Ireland on business was overwhelming at first, but also exhilarating, trying to figure out how things worked. The Libya Palace, one of two main hotels, became my abode of choice. It was always full and there was little point trying to book in advance by telex, the main mode of communication at the time. I realized early on that while the hotel may indeed have been full at certain times, it was "full" at all times according to the front desk staff. They were not paid well and they depended on "selling" rooms for cash to supplement their meager lot. I often paid more to get in than the cost of the room for the first night.

The average big company American found this and many other negotiable items not to his liking. He was used to booking a room that stayed booked, meetings that were on time, and certainly not having to wait a day or even a week to meet a senior executive or minister. Market statistics and information that he would normally have readily to hand were nonexistent here. The Inshalla, Bukra, Malaish, or Arabic "IBM" philosophy, as we called it, was prevalent—Inshalla, "with the help of Allah," Bukra, "tomorrow," and Malaish, "it doesn't matter anyway."

I took a little time to decode the philosophy and ethos and to operate with this in mind, but it caused major indigestion to the Americans. While now in the desert for the first time, many of them were reduced to my level, without significant written research material. Without this basic resource, they were like the half-blind stumbling around without their canes.

I arrived at the hotel front desk from the airport one afternoon to be informed, as expected, that there were no free rooms. I exchanged a knowing glance with the staffer and he proffered the hopeful advice that there might be an opening later in the evening. I showed him my passport to curry initial favour because the Libyans at that time were very partial to the Irish; they thought we were all fellow-travelers of the I.R.A, an organization Colonel Gaddafi had supported with arms. I then moved to an armchair in the lobby, with a prominent view of the front desk.

The lobby was large with a high ceiling that accentuated the feeling of space. The marble floor was covered in places with intricately woven rugs. The walls and ceiling were white, enhancing the feeling of space. Mine was one of a few luxury armchairs that, along with a large sofa, lined one side across from the front desk. There were several exotic trees dotted around the lobby.

I didn't have to wait for long to get the opportunity to ingratiate myself further with the man at the front desk. An aggressive American was haranguing him about his reservation that had mysteriously disappeared. I jumped in to take the part of the Libyan and try to calm the American down. I didn't succeed with the latter but succeeded with my primary objective—to sweeten up "my man." As the afternoon turned to evening, I continued to sit in the armchair, looking serious and sad; however, I had the good fortune to be able to come to the assistance of "my man" at least two more times because of people remonstrating about their disappeared reservations.

I could see, at about 11:00 p.m., that "my man" was preparing to take off for the evening and I began to despair. Then, when I least expected it, he called me over. "Mr. Jermyn, there is another man here from Ireland, he claims he has a reservation, and I have tried to explain we are full. Would you be able to offer him a share of your room?" he said, turning to me with a sly smile.

It took me a moment to understand what was happening before I blurted out, "Of course, he will be welcome, as I know you have a full house." As I got ready to check-in, I slipped a large dinar note into the back of my passport before handing it to him. He was about to open the passport when his boss passed behind him. I froze; in most cases accepting bribes was anathema to the bosses—unless they got them themselves—and "my man" could be in severe trouble if he was caught. I never took my eyes off the passport, and when he handed it back, I opened the back surreptitiously to remove the note. I could not believe it was gone. With the sleight of hand of a card magician, he had removed it unseen in front of me, the boss, and anyone else who may have been watching.

He had also now engineered things such that the other Irishman was full of gratitude to me for allowing him to share my room, while in fact, I was jumping a ride in his. I realized that this other Irishman would not be given the opportunity to check-in, in any case, as "my man" needed a sale at the end of the evening and it was too late to groom this newcomer. I got on well with my compatriot and we spent a whole week together, he still filled with gratitude. Before I left at the end of the week I hadn't the heart to keep up the charade and I owned up to the real story. He took it well and saw the humourous side when I told him how long I had been waiting in the lobby using my stealth tactics with obstreperous potential customers to curry favour with the front desk.

After a week in Tripoli, when it was time to leave for home, I often had to go to great lengths to get there. On this occasion, I called to confirm my flight, to be informed there was no booking. This was not unusual and similar to the hotel situation. Now I had the good fortune to have received a few boarding cards from a friend in Libyan Airlines. At that time, they were laminated so they could be used regularly.

At the airport, I could have gone directly to the departure gates with one of these cards but I was stubborn enough to want to get my suitcase on board too. I lay in wait near one of the check-in desks until the representative temporarily left; I reached over the counter and took a baggage tag. I retreated to the side and put the tag on my bag, then moved along the counter and eased it onto the conveyor belt. In the toilet, I tore out the ticket and put it in my shoe, determined to sit it out on the plane if there was a person-by-person check of tickets for 'gatecrashers,' a not uncommon event at that time. I discovered the ticket-in-the-shoe-trick in Nigeria. In case you were outed and ordered off the plane you had your ticket for future use. I was lucky there was more than one seat free, no check, and I had a relaxed flight to London.

A normal stay in Tripoli.

NEW YORK

43

SETTLING IN

Christine and I arrived in New York in September 1978, having married the previous March and being transferred to the New York office of the Irish Trade Board. I was the envy of many of my colleagues, as New York was regarded as a prime posting. I welcomed the appointment and understood that as much as I liked the Middle East and Africa I could get typecast if I didn't make a move, and what a place to move to. I quickly realized it was a great city if you had youth, health, and money. We had all three and proceeded to have a great time.

We found an apartment on the upper east side between First and York and didn't realize we were in the middle of the beautiful people until we saw a young woman with skin-tight red leather pants towing two large Afghan hounds. My first splurge was a fancy sound system with huge speakers that stood on the ground that I had always wanted but could never afford. I bought records of some of my favourite singers, Jimi Hendrix and Janis Joplin included. I belted the hell out of two speakers with these two. "Color My World" by Chicago was a special gentle love song.

I quickly got used to the directness of New Yorkers. When I answered the phone in the office, they'd ask, "Can I speak to Vincent?"

"I'm sorry, he is not in at the moment," I'd respond.

"What are you sorry about?" the caller would retort.

Sometimes I'd say, "I'm afraid Vincent isn't in at the moment," to which I again got, "What are you afraid of?"

It didn't take long for me to realize that the callers weren't intending to be rude but rather were signaling that they didn't need the Victorian politeness I was raised with.

One evening as we passed the Hilton in midtown, we ran across a big event as limos pulled to the curb and disgorged ladies in finery and men in tuxedos. Walking through this crowd was a young woman in jeans towing a llama behind her. What was remarkable was neither she nor the partygoers took any notice of the other. The quintessential New Yorkers didn't easily surprise or shock each other. They knew little about the broader world and their self-belief was illustrated by a great bumper sticker of the times that said "When ya leave New York, ya ain't going nowhere." Once you passed their hard veneer, they were generous and hospitable and a joy to encounter.

I watched Pope John Paul II on Fifth Avenue as he made a famous visit in the Fall of 1978. The *New York Times* had been on strike, and I have a spoof edition where the headline referred to John Paul John Paul because his predecessor, also John Paul, the smiling Pope, lasted only a month. Some say he was poisoned as he had been talking about giving away some of the Vatican's wealth. John Paul II had come through Ireland on his way to the US and I couldn't help noticing some of the ironies. He had two basic messages for the Irish—the

IRA should stop their violence, and he thanked and praised the people for maintaining good catholic values and their true faith. In the case of the former, the IRA exploded a bomb near the border before he had even left Dublin; in the case of the latter message, as he flew off to the US, the president of Ireland was outed in the media for having a woman additional to his wife. Changing times, indeed.

Aer Lingus, in Dublin, kindly gave Christine an introduction to their New York office. She was taken on and enjoyed her work, being conscientious and loyal. However, her female boss took offence at something that Christine could not figure out. It could have been that Christine was young and having an exciting lifestyle, whereas her boss was single, middle-aged, with limited interests. In any case, she received one of the all-time most interesting comments at review time.

"The best thing I can say about you is your work," said her boss.

In the summer, our apartment was plagued by cockroaches, mainly coming out of the sink in the bathroom. Although we were paying good rent it was no protection and we found out that this scourge existed all over Manhattan. Muhammad Ali did a famous ad for a 'Roach Motel' trap while uttering the immortal line: "Where the roaches check-in but they don't check-out."

They drove Christine crazy, but for myself, I developed a strategy where, if I encountered one in the sink when I was reaching for the soap, and if it didn't take me out of my way, I would hit it. Otherwise, I would not chase after one and thereby allow it to set my agenda. I later developed this into a philosophy for life: don't pursue somebody who has done you harm, as they are then setting your agenda.

44

SOCIAL LIFE

We had a good social life and plenty of discretionary time to travel. We visited Rio de Janeiro and Barbados during our off-time but our more enjoyable trips were the times we drove to the Amish country in nearby Pennsylvania. The austerity of the Amish people, with no electricity or phone and no self-propelled farm machinery, was astounding in the middle of an advanced consumer society. We saw the majestic spectacle of a team of four horses pulling a plough and the little square black horse-drawn buggies travelling on the narrow roads surrounded by cars.

Christine met an immigrant Dutch weaver, Nieltje, who lived in the area, and spent a lot of time with her, as she had started to weave herself. Nieltje wove beautiful items and with great patience showed Christine some techniques. Christine also took up weaving lessons to supplement the lessons she'd received from Nieltje and bought a large Swedish loom. She was well settled and happy in New York and had begun to explore her artistic side.

We had no lack of visitors from Ireland and enjoyed showing them around. One morning when I got up, I had to climb over a body to get into the kitchen, at which time I realized we needed to moderate our open-door policy for staying guests. However, the most memorable visits for us were family visits—Christine's mother, sister, and brother, and my mother, on her own. At one stage, Christine's brother, who had played with the Carrigaline Pipe band, busked with his bagpipes on Fifth Avenue. He did very well partly because the pedestrians were amused by the unusual busking instrument.

My mother's curiosity for such a different environment to what she knew was a joy to behold, and away from her shop in Toormore, we had more time to chat than when I usually visited. I have photographs of us at the top of the World Trade Center. We also took the Circle Line around Manhattan. We walked along the East River near our apartment. St. Bartholomew's, on Park Avenue, for Sunday service, was a high point for her. She was flabbergasted by the contrast with the Altar church in Toormore—the fabulous décor and furnishings, the stained-glass windows, and the large crowd. The only thing in common was the words.

We also drove to Toronto one summer with Christine's mother and sister to meet up with their cousins who lived in Mississauga. We were impressed by the cleanliness of the city and I was particularly impressed by Ontario Place. Little did we realize we would be seeing Toronto again in a few years.

45

BRUISED IN THE BRONX

Transferred from years of wheeling and dealing in the hot climates of the Middle East and Africa, I had been in Manhattan for just over a week. I had never worked with consumer products before, least of all food and drink, and had no direct experience of selling, especially in the US market. I saw this as a challenge.

My predecessor, David, from whom I was taking over the food desk, was very generous with his time and explained my main initial responsibility was to pursue a St. Patrick's Day promotion for Irish food products in some supermarket chain in New York. He had done this the previous year with Sloan's, a small Manhattan-based chain. The results were disastrous. The problem was the promoted products were primarily categorized as specialty, a generous description for most of the tired samples. They neither met the criteria for the main shelves nor had the promotional budgets to back up a shelf listing. When I asked why we were doing this, he told me the boss was stuck on the idea and there was no changing him.

"Who are you?" asked Ed Hoare, chief food buyer for ShopRite supermarkets in the Bronx.

"My name is Bill Jermyn, I am from the Irish Trade Board and I would like to sell you on the idea of a St. Patrick's promotion in all of your stores," I responded.

"Oh, you're Irish?" he said. "My grandmother was Irish," and he sat up with interest in his chair.

"What county was she from?" I asked.

"Cork," he responded.

"That's where I come from too," I said. "It is a beautiful place, you should visit."

"Do they have electricity there now, or does everyone still go around in horse and buggy?" he asked.

And so, we continued for about ten minutes with this inane conversation that seemed to please so many Irish Americans. I relaxed and thought I was winning here at last. I had been with A&P and Grand Union earlier in the week and wiped out after a few minutes in both places. Then Hoare stopped mid-speech, looked at his watch and then down at the products that I had already foolishly spread out on his desk. Knitting his black Irish eyebrows: "Ok, Bill," he said. "Where are the products?"

I ignored his comment, as these were the products. "I have Old Time Irish Marmalade, McCann's Oatmeal, and Gateaux's fruit cake in a tin," I said, as I lifted each in turn. I did not dare venture to the Galway tea with no strings on the bags, and a few more tired-looking specimens. After I'd spent a week of frustration with other supermarkets, the penny was finally dropping—these products had no place in New York supermarkets. In a panic, I reached down to my desert-scuffed briefcase and came up brandishing the only product I had left, a lone bottle of Guinness. "Would you like something decent to drink?" I said.

"You're a nice guy, Bill," he said, as he smiled slightly. "But come back again when you understand the food business here." I had obviously provided him with some entertainment, but he was already late for his next appointment with the guy from Kraft Foods.

I got up from the chair in his tiny prison, picked up my briefcase, and backed in confusion towards the door. As I felt the door at my back, Hoare gestured at his desktop and said, "Take this shit with you." So, I stumbled back, and holding the briefcase open with one hand, began to sweep the products off the desk as quickly as possible with the other. In my blind haste a jar of Laird's Strawberry jam crashed to the floor and I went down on my knees in a stupor, sweeping up the raw red jam and bits of broken glass with both my bare hands and dumping the whole sorry mess into the briefcase, handful by handful. I was humiliated.

It took me a while to recover my confidence, and it took me some time to learn how the food business worked and the difference between specialty and mainstream products. I realized I would have to come up with an attractive deal.

The first component was to offer our 'crap' specialty products on a sale-or-return basis; our promotional events would create commotion in the stores, the better to sell ShopRite's other products. For example, we would arrange store appearances by Floyd Patterson, a boxer, and Carmel Quinn, the entertainer. I glossed over the fact that these were not exactly A-listers anymore, but were all we could afford. To cap it off, we would produce a TV advertisement to run during the promotion.

When I went back to Ed Hoare, I had already mailed him my proposal. First, he laughed and said: “I see you refer to these as ‘crap’ products.”

“Yes,” I said, “I got that idea from you—you actually described them as shit.”

“I’ve never heard that line for selling before,” he said. “You have learned fast, Bill. Let’s do a deal.”

I looked down at my battered briefcase and realized there were better days ahead.

46
ELECTRIC TELEPHONE

In New York, of all places, I had my last experience of the old wind-up phone, long after it had disappeared in most places. This was the late seventies, and while rotary phones were now ubiquitous, there were a few small pockets in Ireland where the wind-up phone and manual exchange still existed. I was in my New York office trying to connect a US food importer by conference call to Lairds, an Irish producer of jam, located in the small town of Drumshanbo, Co. Cavan. The number was Drumshanbo 3.

With the importer on line in conference, the New York telephone operator started an odyssey she had never experienced before. The local operator in Drumshanbo answered her call and tried to contact the marketing manager in the company. She got no reply after prolonged trying. "I know he is there," she said, "I saw him through the window—his office is just across the road. He has me heart scalded; I don't know what's wrong with him but it's nearly impossible to get him to answer. I will go across and rap on his window and tell him there is a call from New York."

I had some banter with the New York operator who had never considered this peculiar form of nurturing as part of her duties. The Drumshanbo operator eventually returned after about five minutes and put an end to our banter. "I pinned him down," she said triumphantly. Very soon he was on the line. Early in the conversation, I made the mistake of joking with him about the operator's performance. He illustrated his displeasure and evidently a continuing dogfight with her. "That bitch has me driven demented," he said. "I have no peace with her sticking her nose into everything." A few moments later the line went dead.

The importer and I decided it would be imprudent to try to reconnect immediately as we figured the street-crossing outreach may not be offered again. I couldn't help looking back with a smile at the innocence of the days of the first "electric telephone" in Toormore, and just like my father, knowing that "no friend of mine would be calling me."

47

SAUSAGE CASINGS TO LIQUEURS

Apart from the St. Patrick's Day Food Promotion where we did go ahead with a TV ad and promotional material, there were two other products that illustrated the diversity of my portfolio.

A Dutchman with a factory in Waterford processed natural beef and lamb sausage casings from animal intestines. He thought there may be a market in the US, sent me some samples, and asked me to get feedback. He advised me Kosher Jewish butcher shops in Brooklyn would be a good place to start. So off I went with a bucket of samples in salt in the trunk of a hired car. Brooklyn then was not trendy and the Jewish butchers were a world apart. I parked the car outside a butcher's shop, opened the trunk, and dragged my bucket of samples into the shop. I approached a man with a long black beard and a dirty outer coat:

"Would you like to check out some natural kosher sausage casings from Ireland?"

"Vot are you talking about?" he responded.

"Sausage casings from Ireland."

"I don't like Holland," he replied.

"Ireland, not Holland," I corrected.

"England, I don't like it either."

"Ireland, not England."

"Vere is Ireland?"

I decided to cut my losses on this one. Many other butchers I approached had little English and communication was also difficult. So, I didn't make much progress. Also, I found out that they didn't want to source their casings outside of New York, never mind from across the Atlantic. Eventually, my research petered out. The samples looked very similar to condoms and I wondered whether I would have been better marketing them as such, with the bonus of being all-natural. I needed a more interesting project.

Emmets Irish Cream launched their drink soon after Baileys. Two senior executives left Baileys' importer to do the marketing for Emmets. I helped them liaise with Emmets and with promotions. Also, I picked up a lot of knowledge of liqueur marketing from the two. The newly launched Baileys and two copycats, Emmets being one, were the highlights of the Irish food and drink portfolio at that time. As mentioned in the St. Patrick's promotion, most of the food products were unsuitable for the market or dated in terms of what the market wanted. I was slowly coming to grips with the fact that my job was not very interesting or productive.

48

DEPRESSION

All was not rosy. In my second year, the Black Dogs of depression returned suddenly and brutally with no obvious external triggers. I spent a period running daily, up and down by the East River in the early mornings, hoping that would help shake them. No such luck. At one stage, Christine helped me get out of bed and dressed, and then accompanied me in a taxi to the office, where I frequently spent a whole morning composing a simple small letter. I was grateful for her loyalty.

It was a New York psychiatrist who drew a sine curve on a piece of paper and showed me that "manic" meant up and "depressive" meant down. She was shocked I didn't know this was the essence of manic depression or bipolar disorder and pointed out the more you pushed being high with increased energy, little sleep, and grandiose thoughts, the more you risked going over the top and down to depression. I had done this before. I had heard the diagnosis previously, but hadn't internalized the full meaning. I was as low as on previous occasions, with a complete loss of confidence; I couldn't find joy in anything and found it hard to concentrate. Like before, I could not see any possibility of a break in the clouds in the future and felt embarrassed in front of my colleagues. Not only did I not fully understand the illness, its causes, prevention, and cure, there was a stigma around mental illness. Over time, I had developed the dubious skill of hiding my feelings from others, apart from those close to me.

We were due to transfer back to Dublin in late September 1980, as Jimmy Carter's presidency was coming to an end. We went on our last vacation, camping down east to Maine. The weather was cooler than the summer heat in Manhattan but the countryside and shoreline were spectacular. We feasted on clam chowder and lobsters everywhere. Mercifully, the bark of the Black Dogs was easing by the time we returned to New York and prepared for home.

I had nearly fully recovered by the time we returned to Dublin in 1980, and to the head office of the Irish Trade Board. I think a contributory external reason that triggered the depression may have been that I harboured dreams of staying in the US at one stage, but was unable to come up with viable options in the limited time period. The uncertainty was destabilizing and my self-esteem took a hit from yet again being unable to make up my mind about what I wanted and to plan accordingly. Also, compared to what I had done in the Middle East and Africa, the job of trying to promote unsuitable products was soul-destroying.

Previously, I had assumed after each bout of depression that was the end and it would not return in the future. I didn't inform myself of the details and I didn't take medication consistently. I realized now that this was a condition I might have to deal with for life. One of the effects of this depression, in particular, was that hardly a day went by without me looking over my shoulder in expectation of another joust with the Black Dogs. This ate at my self-esteem and self-confidence.

While having depressive bouts intermittently, I have luckily experienced manic episodes on only a few occasions. Hypomania is a term used by psychiatrists to describe the upside of bipolar mood disorder, when one is not extremely manic. Typically, in this state, I felt all-powerful and my creativity increased. Christine and friends found this hypomanic activity more difficult to deal with than when I was depressed. As someone said, "it's like pissing in your pants; you get a lovely warm feeling but then there is all hell to pay."

DUBLIN

49

RETURN

After I regained my pre-depression self-confidence, I hit a lucky streak. I had a long four-year period where, essentially, I was back to an active and normal life.

We moved back into our first house in Ballinteer. After a few months of familiarizing ourselves with the market, we decided to go for a bigger house and nearer to our old haunts in Blackrock. We bought in Priory Drive, Stillorgan, and sold Ballinteer. We had bought Ballinteer just over two years earlier and this was the best real estate buy we ever made. We were very happy to be amongst our friends and familiar surroundings again, close to Avondale.

We were able to pick up again with most of our old friends. However, a few were not able to deal with the fact we had lived somewhere else and our views had changed on some things, like Ireland's and the US's places in the world. I found some also had little curiosity about how we lived so we could only connect with the experiences they had while we were away. While we had less to do with those, we acquired some very good new friends. They fitted the profile of those who had either lived overseas, like ourselves, or international people in Dublin.

We had two cars—the good one, Alfasud, and an old Fiat wreck that had rust and holes in numerous places. Needless to say, the Fiat was for me and, later, Bucky the dog.

My father and mother came to visit and inspect the house. As I was showing my father around, I told him that the closet inside the front door with a basin and toilet could be classified as a second bathroom, but the real status symbol then was the third bathroom. To achieve this would require relinquishing a bedroom or extending at the back; either would involve a heavy cost. The only comment he made was: "Sure, Bill, you can only shit in one place at a time."

In 1982 we decided we should either renovate the cottage that my parents had given me in Toormore or sell it. Sentiment was against sale; this was where I'd lived for part of my childhood. We couldn't afford a total upgrade; we replaced the windows and the roof and put an extension at the back with a bathroom. It was very livable and all at a low cost. We got great use of the cottage and it is in our possession to this day.

Life was good. After a few months back in Dublin it felt as if we had never been away. It was good also to be able to spend time with my parents. Christine's mother and other family members visited at various times too. Every time I drove from Dublin and arrived at the sea at the entrance to Toormore, with the Altar Stone on the left, I felt at home again. The surroundings of rock, wildflowers, and sea were always a relief from city living. I never wanted to move anywhere again.

50
BABY BOY

I arrived home late from the pub on the night that Christine got the news she was pregnant. She was upset that I'd not been present to celebrate the news. She was in bed and told me as I got in. I was very upset and felt I had let her down and let myself down as well. I made a mental promise to cut down on my pub visits as I realized I was indulging in a prolonged adolescence.

The prospect of becoming a father did not register at this stage. This took days on a slow burn to sink in. I speculated whether the baby might look like Christine or me. We didn't particularly worry whether it was a girl or boy, and in those days, finding out in advance was not an option. We had a spare bedroom but did not paint it any colours. Both of us were in awe of the miracle ahead and were superstitious about too much advance planning.

I was exposed at an early stage to Christine's gynecologist. He had upset her by being vague about delivery plans and she came home crying. He had told her also he would like to meet me before the birth. The time came about two weeks in advance. After some small talk and more vagueness about delivery arrangements, delivered with a condescending style, he demonstrated an arrogance that I could see had upset Christine. This sense of not treating the patient as an equal was not uncommon in the medical profession. I decided it was time to soften him up:

"I'm a professional too so I see myself and you no different to a plumber—will the job be done, and well?"

Giving the plumber analogy a moment to sink in I continued: "We would like a natural birth and no inducing for the convenience of the doctors."

"What do you mean?" he retorted. "Everything is done in the interest of the mother."

"Why then in Holles Street Hospital, the biggest baby factory in Europe, is there a big drop off in births at the weekends, especially in summer?" I asked.

No reply.

My next exposure to him was when he called to say he recommended Christine go in to be induced. "Is it essential?" I queried.

"Well, it is my recommendation," he said.

I realized that if we ignored his recommendation, we could blame ourselves if anything went wrong.

We compromised; we didn't go in on the day he recommended, but a few days later, and Christine had a natural birth. When she started labour pains, we sat on either side of the bed with our legs dangling and our backs together like bookends. As she broke into breathing exercises, I followed with the same movements. At a certain point, a nurse asked "Would you leave now for a short time?"

"I suppose this is in case I would see my wife naked," I responded with a smile.

The hospital was relatively new to allowing fathers present for births. They were still at the stage of allowing rather than welcoming, while thwarting when possible.

The nurse assured me she would call me from the waiting room so I could be there for the birth, which Christine wanted. After some time, I sensed something had gone wrong and I walked along the passageway to the birthing room double doors. I pushed in the doors to find I'd just caught the end of the performance that was perfectly handled by the midwife. Having promised he would be there, the gynecologist arrived when the job was done. I was entranced, counted the baby boy's fingers and toes, and marveled at the miracle.

The next few days were a blur while Christine was in the hospital. I felt different; I had never envisaged having children but now that it had happened, it felt perfectly natural. We still hadn't decided on a name as Christine got ready to leave the hospital, although we had been under a lot of pressure from the officials to do so. I was more interested in the ten fingers and toes than a name. As we stood in the hospital lobby, a nurse told us if we didn't name him then we would have to go to register him at the city office. This extra bureaucracy didn't appeal to either of us so we decided on the spot to go with David. It was an easy choice as it was my dead brother's name. It felt good to put it back in use again. As we drove home, I felt a sense of extra responsibility and was conscious that this was the beginning of the next generation.

51

BUCKY

Bucky Dent was a New York Yankees baseball star in the late seventies. My wife had gotten very attached to baseball, and to Dent in particular—something about his thighs, I believe, although I claim no expertise in what turns women on in that department. On our return to Dublin, and after David was born, I felt we needed a dog to validate and complete the new family. Apart from this, my brothers and I had a dog when we were children and we got great mileage from him—tugging, pulling, jumping on, and generally abusing him daily.

We were on a visit to Toormore, when a man in Gabe's Pub in Ballydehob offered me two pups for free. With some trepidation, I took both but felt better when I was able to offload one on my mother. They were siblings, both completely black, crazy, typical West Cork mongrels of indeterminate lineage. My best guess was a mix of collie, springer, and local terrier. As is often the case with mongrels, they were sleek in build; both had very handsome faces. We called our dog Bucky.

While I only got to West Cork a few times a year, the dogs remembered each other every time and I spent many hours watching them racing each other in the fields. They both had an incredible ability to change direction abruptly, in full flight, and leave the other floundering trying to follow. Equally, when I stood in their paths and tried to put a hand on them, I was always left catching air.

Bucky settled in well to urban life and I took him many places without a lead. He went everywhere with me in the Fiat wreck; he would sit upright in the passenger seat and was a general custodian. Once I told a friend at work he could borrow the car to deliver a message, but he came back fifteen minutes later to tell me Bucky was in the car and wouldn't let him near it. How could poor Bucky know the car wasn't worth defending?

He had never impressed me with any sense of responsibility beyond eating his fill and banishing stray cats. However, when my wife began to walk out with the child in a baby carriage, I noticed that Bucky always wanted to go. She told me he circled the baby carriage when any strangers passed, and sometimes growled if they stopped—and this from a dog who had previously never shown an iota of bad temperament to the family.

Later, I saw this for myself when our young boy walked with his grandmother by the shore, on a visit to Toormore. There was a very long sandy beach before getting to the water and Bucky would not allow the grandmother to take the boy alone—he accompanied them the whole way to the sea, entered with them, and stayed until they were finished. Again, he went up in my estimation of him.

He got into the habit of chasing female dogs when the scent was right. This meant that he was often absent from home for several nights in a row. He always came back, never the worse for wear, although sometimes he would sleep things off in his bed for a few days. Once, during one of these escapades, I got a call at my office in the late afternoon: "Are you Mr. Jermyn?" said an older female voice.

"Yeees," I said carefully, wondering what sin had I committed now.

"Your dog has been hit by a car, and is not showing any signs of life," said the woman. "We are with him at the side of Mount Merrion Avenue." She must have got my name and number from the identity tag.

"I am on my way," I said. "Don't move him until I arrive." My heart dropped when I drove up Mount Merrion Avenue. A large group of women surrounded the dog, who was prone on the sidewalk. I braced for the worst.

"He was hit by a car," said one of the women.

"Bucky, Bucky, Bucky," I called. He raised his head slowly on hearing my voice, picked himself up even more slowly, began to struggle to the car, and before I could move to help him, he crawled into his usual place in the passenger seat. The Lazarus-like resurrection won a round of applause from the women. I was so proud of him as I gently placed him in his bed at home. Of course, the important thing was he did not show a sign of weakness in front of the outsiders. It took him three days before he emerged again.

52

OFFICE

I had a very fulfilling professional life back in Dublin as I was now a section manager, and I was managing staff. I took this aspect very seriously and studied and took courses. For a short time after my return, I was section manager for textiles and print & packaging. On the textiles side I have fond memories of a visit to an exhibition in Paris. My expert colleague, Marie, had the patience to try to educate me. I learned how the fabric season is six months ahead of the fashion season, which is in turn six months ahead of the retail season. The process of deciding the seasonal choice of colours was capricious.

After a reshuffling of our department, I was put back in charge of construction services. As well as Marie, I had Gerry and Richard, two of the smartest men I have worked with, and it was my good fortune that we all became friends as well as colleagues. Fred, another good man, joined later. When, eventually, Gerry transferred to Sydney and Richard to Paris, I knew a special era was over.

My two support staff, Teresa and Fiona, were great and suffered gamely through some of my peculiar habits. I had grappled with the challenge to ensure clients had a satisfactory experience when they called. At that time too many people around Dublin had a practice where support staff would interrogate the caller for his name and after a short time revert by saying the person they wanted isn't in or isn't available when it was obvious that neither of these statements was true. I eventually came up with the following suggested response for my staff when I was busy:

"Bill has *asked* not to be disturbed." This subtlety didn't stoop to lying and also gave the client and the staff member the responsibility to negotiate whether I *should* be disturbed.

Sean had been promoted to chief executive before I went to New York. I still had a great relationship with him forged in the days we'd worked together, but I might now go weeks or months in between talking to him. I was careful not to abuse our friendship by trying to involve him in any normal ongoing issues. However, a friend told me that many of my colleagues thought I had the ear of the chief executive and so they were careful when dealing with me.

For example, at the more trivial level, nobody said anything when I took to locking my office door at times when I did not wish to be disturbed, and I communicated with my secretary by way of a series of knocks and papers under the door. In fact, my boss nearly broke his nose one day when he assumed the door was open. Also, I frequently brought Bucky to the office and he minded the car during the day. Sometimes I brought him into the office where he lay happily under the desk. Once, I kept him in the office when I had a client visiting. I was very friendly with this client and so there would be no embarrassment if Bucky acted up. Unfortunately, at some stage I felt a warm feeling against my leg; Bucky had gotten nervous under the desk and had started to pee. Fortunately, my office was situated close to the elevator and I was able to get him out quickly without too much damage, and without being noticed, at least by many.

I didn't realize it then, but I had accidentally fallen into the perfect corporate position if your main objective is to acquire and deliver a level of expertise, rather than move up the management ladder. The key here is to have a mentor who can help by offering you space. In return, you provide the mentor objective advice when he seeks it. Most people at his table are looking for his job or saying what they think he wants to hear. You, because of your focus, have no interest beyond doing your best to tell the objective truth. In my case, Sean had known over the years I was a straight shooter, and when he asked for my opinion, he knew it came without strings. In return, I don't think he actively tracked my welfare, but for sure the few power brokers, like exist in all large organizations, were afraid he might notice if they tried to attack me. They knew I could seek his assistance, so I got space to ply my expertise, such as it was.

My last big event involvement before leaving Dublin again was as a co-organizer of a Jumbo Trade Mission to Saudi Arabia in the fall of 1983. Previous trade missions to Saudi would have involved no more than twenty companies. Sean had asked Owen, the main organizer, and me to go for broke and get as many as we could. When we got near to thirty, he asked us to stop but we were slow to comply and eventually we had close on fifty participants.

The trade mission was the biggest ever and very successful in terms of business signed and raising the Irish profile. This was the culmination of nearly four years back at head office where I had much professional development and success, made a lot of new friendships, and enjoyed myself immensely.

53

SERVICES ENGINEER

Before leaving the workplace, I want to mention two characters from outside of the mainstream who left a strong impression on me—Timmy O'Hanlon , Services Engineer, and May Noone, Tea Lady.

"The fools, the fools," said Timmy. "The Wyndham Land Act, 1903, gave them their freedom, but they couldn't see it." He was referring to the first British Act that gave the Irish the freedom to own their own land, and so according to Timmy, with a certain amount of logic, there was no need for the 1916 rebellion, or the War of Independence.

Timmy was in full flight at the bar in the Merrion Inn, with his slow articulation of the myopia of Irish nationalists. In his early sixties, he was tall with his hair slicked back and a gaunt face. I joined him for a drink many evenings after work in our nearby office, where he was employed as the services engineer. Our other drinking companion was Walter Connor, head of a unit of an engineering and construction conglomerate.

Timmy was born and grew up in Castlemagner, a small town in North Cork. His family had impeccable nationalist credentials. He had to leave to get work, at a time when there were few jobs outside of farming, and poverty was rife. I am not sure how he decided to go to Belfast and found himself a job in Harland & Wolf, the shipbuilders of the Titanic. In any case, he spent most of the second World War working there and went through a very unusual metamorphosis for a southern Irish nationalist. He emerged as a dyed-in-the-wool unionist, possibly even to the right of Ian Paisley, in terms of his allegiance to the crown. At best I can surmise, his unusual conversion was in part due to the fact that the unionists in Belfast gave him a job when there were none available in the Republic. Also, he found the worldview of nationalism at that time to be narrow and limited.

At some point after this come-to-Jesus process, the nationalists in Castlemagner invited him as the guest of honour for the unveiling of a statue to his IRA uncle, who was a big honcho in the movement. He refused to go.

One of my bosses suggested to me that if I wanted to progress in the organization I should not be seen to be drinking with Timmy, the humble service engineer. The same manager had previously commented on the state of my car, and the fact that I frequently brought my dog to work in it. I didn't think that Timmy's work status had any relevance to the quality of his conversation, and felt validated by our buddy Walter, who was a CEO and flew and crashed his own plane! What intrigued me about Timmy was his interesting and iconoclastic views about nationalism and the British empire, at a time when I found it difficult to find some original thinking.

Our drinking sessions were in the early eighties and straddled the time of the Falklands war. "She'll show them," said Timmy, referring to Margaret Thatcher and the Argentinians.

Walter and I had great amusement laughing at him for his extremism, but there was no budging him on his devotion to Thatcher and the UK.

54

TEA LADY

"Tea up boys, tea up," Mary cried as she pushed her trolley into our office at 10:30. a.m. every morning. Her arrival was as regular and timely as the morning Angelus call to worship on the radio, the latter to which we responded with less zeal. I don't remember Mary's last name. I was trying to take in so much about my new environment at my first job at the Department of Post and Telegraphs that I don't remember much about her, but I remember the trolley, and what it signified for our office in the early seventies. No matter what we were doing, or whether we were working hard, although this was unusual, we all immediately downed tools and congregated around her.

The Tea Lady was an integral part of our office routine and ritual. We took our mugs back to our desks and continued our analysis of whatever problems of the world we were solving. We could spend up to thirty minutes in discussion before returning to work. This ritual was repeated in the afternoon.

In my next job with Arthur Andersen, needless to say, in this US culture, there was no Tea Lady—we made our own in a fancy kitchen. No time to stop and talk, no time to go to the bathroom, everything was important and urgent, and everyone kept a time sheet. Although I learned a lot, I got restless in a culture that took itself so seriously and put inordinate emphasis on the God of Mammon.

When I joined the Irish Trade Board, I was back again to a Tea Lady culture. I had missed the typical strong personality, her aura, and her strategic position in the organizations of the seventies. Most of these ladies had been around for years, had the ear of senior management, and were not shy about reporting a young pup who did not show enough respect.

The first Tea Lady I encountered in the Irish Trade Board was called Ma Foley—nobody knew her first name, and dared not ask. She was bent over like a question mark and wore nondescript black clothing, displaying many of the higher order qualities of a witch, including being cantankerous and in bad mood at all times. She had been the housekeeper for a previous chief executive, and he parachuted her into this job when he was downsizing his home, probably to avoid her vitriol at losing her job. She ruled the trolley with an iron urn. We daren't ask for something special, and complaint was out of the question. Her carrot and stick techniques involved offering individual cookies to her favourite young men (not women!). The problem was she produced these cookies from the side pocket of her work coat, which was as unwashed as her hands. If one was getting too much of "the cookie," the challenge was to incur her mild wrath. For example, spilling the tea could be enough to be struck off the cookie list, but not enough to have her reporting upstairs.

When we moved to a new office building, Ma Foley was thrown under the bus. I never learned what happened to her. I suppose it fitted the mythical image of her profession to give the impression of appearing from the mists of nowhere and disappearing back just as easily. In any case, the new lady was May Noone, small, a little overweight, and white hair to match her white coat. She was a force of nature—upbeat, talkative, sociable, with a great sense of humour. I warmed to her immediately.

May came from a fine house inherited from her family in nearby Sandymount. She expounded on many subjects, and her laugh could be heard before the trolley came into sight. She loved personal chats with anyone who was prepared to engage. However, she had a problem—her husband, Paddy, had moved in after marriage, "hung his cap," and never did a day's work thereafter. And, to make matters worse, her son, who lived at home, had acquired a similar allergy to work. She often complained to me about this: "Bill, they don't believe in the auld Victorian ethic of hard work being necessary for salvation, especially when there is someone else to take care of them."

"I know, May," I said. "There are many women stuck trying to cure this allergy and there is no easy antidote."

She joked about her problem, but I could see it was causing distress. One day in June, she arrived in the office in a foul mood. I asked her what was wrong.

"Ah Jasus, Bill when I went home yesterday afternoon Paddy was squealing like a stuck pig. He had been sunbathing on a deckchair in the back garden and d'ye know what happened? He fell asleep, got burnt, and was red as a tomato. And he's complaining to me! It's my fault, of course! Jasus, Bill, I woulda got better in a fecking lucky bag!" A lucky bag at that time contained a few useless trinkets and was bought by children for about two pence.

The role is now long dead as a dodo in Dublin. While Joseph Addison wrote in the eighteenth century about the "socializing, civilizing aspect of a country Sunday," in my early working days, Tea Ladies served a similar function in the office, had influence beyond their status, but rarely received the recognition they deserved.

55
NEW HORIZON

I had been three years at the head office of the Irish Trade Board in Dublin, so the possibility of a relocation was on the horizon. My friend, Jim, who was well up on the internal workings of the organization, came to me one day for a chat.

"While I know you are happy in your current position, Bill, after three years you could be in line soon for another overseas transfer."

I hadn't even begun to think about this.

"The next three postings to be filled are Lagos, Moscow, and Toronto," he said.

"Why can't I continue what I'm doing?" I said.

"You know, Bill, there is the practice of rotation and our contractual obligation to accept. Also, because you were lucky enough to get away with not going to Glasgow, you may find it harder to avoid a transfer you don't like a second time," he said.

I had a sinking feeling as I understood his logic. If I didn't pay attention, I could be asked to move to a non-ideal office. I had been happy in Dublin and had hoped not to be sent overseas again.

"The reason I am speaking to you now is that you know Lagos and Moscow are arsehole locations, for different reasons, and you have already served enough time in some strange places. I would suggest you keep your eyes open and put your name in for Toronto," Jim said.

I had visited Lagos a few times, where a trip from the airport to downtown could take six hours because of traffic congestion and there were open sewers in the middle of some streets. Also, the level of graft was unbelievable. Nigeria was a large oil producer but the riches did not seem to get down to the citizens. I shuddered at the thought of living there. While I had not been to Moscow, I had heard enough about the system and business methods to also have no desire to get any closer.

"Toronto is a great place, Bill, and I know you will thrive there," he said.

Jim wasn't just speaking theoretically; he had spent four happy years there.

I went home to discuss this with Christine. While we hadn't even thought about moving again, we realized that a compelling reason was the weak economy, which was in bad shape (interest rates and inflation around 20%). It would be a good time to take four years out on the assumption that it couldn't be worse when we returned. Also, we were young enough to consider one last overseas move.

Without too much more thought, I indicated my interest in Toronto to a senior member of the appointments committee, and then promptly forgot about it. Towards the end of the summer in 1983, I got notice one day that I had been appointed to Toronto on a four-year contract.

So, for the second time, we would pack up and make arrangements to move overseas. The cars had to be sold and the house rented. Our move to Toronto also meant a sad parting with our Bucky. However, he was ending up in an ideal home for his outdoor pursuits. My friend, Tom, the farmer in West Cork, agreed to take him. He would be joining two Pyrennian Mountain Dogs, a whippet, and a mongrel. He would be free to play and roam in the fields to his heart's content. I mourned his presence for a long time, as did Christine. I often tried to imagine him roaming unimpeded on the farm and free of the intrusion of cars with which he had an issue in Dublin.

There was one spanner in the works—we were initially scheduled to leave sometime in October, but I was part of a newly-formed services department headed up by Colm, who was my boss way back when I had the problem with the Glasgow office appointment. It was a pleasure to work for him again and that he was my last boss before leaving Dublin. There were a few things he wanted completed before I left. This situation continued into 1984, and apart from anything else, Christine was pregnant again and she would not be allowed to fly after early March. I think this was what finally convinced him to let me go.

I was surprised when Sean called me to his office one afternoon in early 1984, just before I departed. When I entered his office, he left his desk and motioned me to sit at his round meeting table. He opened one of the closets at the side of the room and pulled out a bottle of vodka and two glasses. There was little small talk before he said: "I haven't told anyone else yet, but I will be leaving shortly. I'm telling you now because you are about to take off to Toronto."

I was shocked.

He followed up quickly: "Now that I'm leaving, you are on your own, I won't be here to protect you anymore."

I tried to tell him how much I respected him but I didn't do a very good job because I was still trying to come to grips with his news.

"I will be eternally grateful that you rescued me after my depression and gave me exciting responsibilities," I said. "And don't worry, I don't do stunts like taking off my shirt in the office anymore, but I appreciate you keeping an eye on me over the years."

I had tears in my eyes leaving his office as I remembered the good times and shared experiences. That was the end of a great relationship, professional and personal.

We departed Dublin for Toronto on Saturday, March 3, 1984. I was thirty-four and wondered what life would bring next.

56
EPILOGUE

By the time I left Ireland, I was skeptical of all religions, especially those of Christian denomination. I frequently tormented the zealous by reminding them that, while Jesus was most probably a good guy, he couldn't be responsible for all those who agreed with him. However, I remained a "cultural" Protestant. I became aware of the danger of "isms" at the extreme, for example, Nationalism and Unionism, leading to violence. The influence of other "isms," Catholicism and Protestantism, for example, intertwined with the political "isms" adding fuel to the fire for an abstract concept of being Irish.

These views, as well as temperament and experience, made me part of the "other," and an outsider in many ways. I had developed a strong sense of localized identity—a Toormore and West Cork man first, Cork man second, and an Irishman a poor third. Being fiercely local made me totally international at the same time; I understood and easily empathized with other regional communities and people who loved their own places, all over the world. The sheep farmer in Sichuan Province and I would understand each other. I am wary of all "isms," especially the trappings of nationalism. I would not wish to die for Ireland but I would, if necessary, for Toormore and West Cork. The 'ism' I respect is regionalism, which brings a sense of place, stability, respect and connection to the wider world.

I have done my share of swimming against the current and will continue to do so. I emigrated to Canada rather than return to Dublin at the end of my contract with the Irish Trade Board. It was a difficult decision as there was merit on both sides. We were very comfortable in the multicultural city of Toronto, which exuded energy and excitement. Having moved house a few times, we settled in the Roncesvalles area, where I have developed a new regional affinity.

I visit Toormore nearly every year, even though most of the pursuits of my youth are only memories. The montbretia, fuchsia, and heather still flower as brightly, and the sea continues its metronomic pounding on the rocks and beaches. Yes, "a savage loves his native shore," said an Irish poet, James Orr, and it will always be home for me.

ACKNOWLEDGEMENTS

I owe a great debt to Paula Turner, Aviva Sinuk, Karen Lavut, Ali Afkham, and Nella Pontillo, in our writers' group. Your variety of ethnic backgrounds helped put a perspective on my own. You put up with reviewing most of my stories and made many good suggestions. Special thanks to Nella who, as well as encouragement, did a preliminary edit. I wouldn't have got this far without all of you and I value your friendship too.

I am grateful to Beth Kaplan who first gave me the courage to write this memoir, and for her continuing mentorship and editing the final manuscript.

I thank Louise Stahl for her excellent work as a proof editor and Megan Hilaire and Jenny Chandler, of Elite Authors, for coordinating the cover design and interior layout.

I am grateful also to the Junction Writers group and, Brian D'Souza in particular, who never ceased to push and prod me when I didn't believe I could do it. Also, Susan Britton made a valuable contribution and reviewed the early manuscript.

A special thank you to Bernadette Gabay Dyer for your constant encouragement.

My family is precious and this is partly for them: David & Anna, Peter, Andrew & Sally, and grandchildren Ellie and Henry.

Thanks to you, my long-suffering wife, Christine. You put up with all the time involved in the writing. I promise I will no longer have an excuse for not doing the jobs I should.

And finally, I would like to pay tribute to all the great characters in the memoir. I am blessed to have met them, that they were part of my life, and without whom there would be no book.

Manufactured by Amazon.ca
Bolton, ON